Y0-AFP-193

BOOK OF EXTREME FACTS 2012

BOOK OF EXTREME FACTS 2012

Written by
Matt Forbeck and Kris Oprisko

Edited by
Kris Oprisko

Design by
Tom B. Long

Cover by
Gabriel Rodriguez

Art by
**Brian Miroglio, Marc Rueda,
Sagar Forniés, Mariano Saura Copete,
Albert Carreres, Guillermo Perez,
Yair Herrera, German Torres**

Special Thanks To
Howard Jonas

ISBN: 978-1-60010-940-9

14 13 12 11   1 2 3 4

IDW®

Ted Adams, CEO & Publisher
Greg Goldstein, Chief Operating Officer
Robbie Robbins, EVP/Sr. Graphic Artist
Chris Ryall, Chief Creative Officer/Editor-in-Chief
Matthew Ruzicka, CPA, Chief Financial Officer
Alan Payne, VP of Sales

Become our fan on Facebook **facebook.com/idwpublishing**
Follow us on Twitter **@idwpublishing**
Check us out on YouTube **youtube.com/idwpublishing**
www.IDWPUBLISHING.com

BOOK OF EXTREME FACTS 2012. AUGUST 2011. FIRST PRINTING. Book of Extreme Facts © 2011 Idea and Design Works, LLC. All Rights Reserved. IDW Publishing, a division of Idea and Design Works, LLC. Editorial offices: 5080 Santa Fe St., San Diego, CA 92109. Any similarities to persons living or dead are purely coincidental. With the exception of artwork used for review purposes, none of the contents of this publication may be reprinted without the permission of Idea and Design Works, LLC. Printed in Korea.
IDW Publishing does not read or accept unsolicited submissions of ideas, stories, or artwork.

TABLE OF CONTENTS

Book of Extreme Facts 2012

Chapter 1 – Sports / Youth Sports 5

Chapter 2 – Extreme Records 29

Chapter 3 – Weather 43

Chapter 4 – The World....................................57

Chapter 5 – Animals 71

Chapter 6 – Machines 85

Chapter 7 – Science 99

Chapter 8 – Extreme People 113

Chapter 9 – Buildings & Construction 127

Chapter 10 – The Ancient World................141

Chapter 11 – Games & Entertainment 155

LETTER FROM THE EDITOR

Dear Readers,

Bigger, stronger, faster, MORE... we humans have always been drawn to extremes. The out-of-the-ordinary, freakish, and outlandish have fascinated from the beginning of time, and today is no exception. In the **BOOK OF EXTREME FACTS 2012**, we present the most compelling of these in a fun, fast-paced format that we know you will enjoy.

Each chapter of this book presents a collection of facts and records that will make your brain burst in disbelief. **UNBREAKABLE** boxes indicate records that have stood the test of time, or are so far and above the norm as to appear almost unbeatable. Similarly, the **WHO'S GOT NEXT?** boxes identify records that are ripe for the picking. **NEWS YOU CAN USE** boxes highlight helpful hints, or things you can try yourself.

While this inaugural edition of the **BOOK OF EXTREME FACTS** is rich with amazing information, our hope is that future volumes will feature even more amazing records set by our readers... that means YOU! Get crazy, get creative, get involved, and be a world record holder. You set the standard, and we will tell the world. Refer to the final page of each chapter to find out how to submit records that just may get you into these pages next year.

In the meantime, enjoy the book... and always remember to **KEEP IT EXTREME!**

Sincerely,

Kris Oprisko
Editor
BOOK OF EXTREME FACTS

CHAPTER 1
SPORTS

Most Successful Windsurfer

BJØRN DUNKERBECK of the Canary Islands has won the world windsurfing championships 35 times. He is twelve-time Professional Windsurfers Association (PWA) Overall World Champion (1988-1999), twelve-time PWA Race World Champion (1988-1999), and seven-time PWA Wave World Champion (1990, 1992, 1993, 1994, 1995, 1999, 2001). In addition, he won the PWA Freestyle World Championships in 1998 as well as the PWA Speed World Championships in 1994 and has scored more than 100 single PWA World Cup victories.

◀...The Fastest Man on Water

After two sessions (November and January) in which he improved his own performance to approach the world record (48.70 knots; 56.043 mph) held since 2005 by Finian Maynard of the Virgin Islands, **ANTOINE ALBEAU** broke the speed sailing record on March 5, 2008. With a top speed of 49.09 knots (56.492 mph), he became not only the fastest windsurfer on the planet over the 500m long run (the sprint distance in speed sailing), but also the fastest sail-powered man as well.

......Long Distance

RAPHAELLA LE GOUVELLO of France windsurfed across the Pacific Ocean, concluding the trip on November 3, 2003. Le Gouvello windsurfed solo from Lima, Peru, to Tahiti in 89 days on a specially designed board that used solar and wind power to operate navigation devices and a radio. During her 5,000-mile maritime marathon, Le Gouvello had to deal with cold weather, huge swells, and close encounters with sharks, seals, and baracudas.

UNBREAKABLE

Consecutive Footbag Kicks

Everyone who's kicked around a footbag, either by themselves or with friends, has tried to keep the footbag going as long as they could. But some people's foot-feats seem almost beyond belief! **CONSTANCE CONSTABLE & TRICIA GEORGE** hold the Women's Doubles Footbag Consecutive kick record of 34,543, while **TRICIA GEORGE & GARY LAUTT** posted an Open Doubles record of 132,011 kicks! In the individual category, **CONSTANCE CONSTABLE** rules the Women's Singles with 24,713 and **TED MARTIN** the overall Open Singles category, kicking the footbag 63,326 consecutive times in 8 hours, 50 minutes, and 42 seconds.

Source: http://www.pwaworldtour.com

Individual 3-3-3 & 3-6-3 Sport Stacking

Starting from its California birthplace, sport stacking is a rapidly expanding youth sport that challenges its participants to create and disassemble pyramids of plastic cups in the fastest time possible. The numbers refer to how many cups are used to create a stack: 3-3-3 means 3 stacks of 3 cups each, while 3-6-3 consists of a 6-cup tower flanked by two 3-cup towers.

Individual 3-3-3 Stack – 1.72 seconds
- **KENNETH LAIO**
  Nashville, TN
  2010 WSSA World Sport Stacking Championships

Individual 3-6-3 Stack – 2.08 seconds
- **KENNARD GARDNER**
  Glen Burnie, MD
  2010 WSSA Maryland State Sport Stacking Championships

WHO'S GOT NEXT?

Timed 3-6-3 Relay Stacking

The relay Sport Stacking event combines the skills of the other disciplines with the further complication of having a four-person team. Each team member must do their best to achieve the fastest time!

Timed 3-6-3 Relay – 12.41 seconds
Team USA:
- **JOHN HARDEN**
  Statesboro, GA
- **LAWRENCE MACEREN**
  Freehold, NJ
- **LUKE MYERS**
  Eden Prairie, MN
- **STEVEN PURUGGANAN**
  Longmeadow, MA

Women's Outdoor Boot Throwing

Born in rural Scandanavia and also very popular in New Zealand, boot throwing is a playful sport pitting competitors against each other to determine who can chuck a rubber boot the farthest distance. Competitors now hail from countries such as Finland, Estonia, Germany, Italy, Sweden, and Poland. While the sport started informally, there are now World Championships held each year. The women's world record is held by **ELINA UUSTALO** of Konnevesi, Finland. Elina managed to heave a gumboot 53.9698 yards (49.35 m) in Leppävirta, Finland.

Men's Outdoor Boot Throwing

Modern boot throwing competitions use a standard boot for each competitor. The boot is gripped from the top, and the thrower gains force for the throw by using an approach that is a mixture of discus and javelin, incorporating a 10- to 15-meter run-up followed by one to five spins. This results in an extremely long throw, none longer among men than the world record toss of an amazing 73.611 yards (67.31 m), set in Leppävirta, Finland, by **JUKKA VESTERINEN** of Heinävesi, Finland.

Most Beaned Baseball Player

Imagine stepping in the batter's box to face a major league pitcher… only to have the pitch slam right into you! Getting beaned is no joke, as the unlucky souls who hold these records can testify. The lifetime leader in this category is **HUGHIE JENNINGS,** a turn-of-the-century player who took 287 hits. In the modern era, Houston's **CRAIG BIGGIO** is a close second with 285. And consider **MINNIE MINOSO,** who played in the '50s & '60s with the White Sox and Indians-he holds the record for Most Total Seasons (9) and Most Consecutive Seasons (6) leading the Major League, as well as the American League Record of leading for 10 seasons. That's gotta hurt!

Most World Series Home Runs

To reach the very pinnacle of Major League Baseball, you've got to win the World Series. And on that grand stage, the great rise to another level. Fielders reach into themselves to make diving catches, and sluggers do what they do best—hit home runs. No one has hit more lifetime World Series home runs than **MICKEY MANTLE'S** 18 for the Yankees. **BABE RUTH** and **REGGIE JACKSON,** both Yankees as well, share the record for most homers in a game with 3… but Babe did it twice, in both 1926 and 1928. And **REGGIE JACKSON,** not to be outdone, holds the astounding mark of 4 home runs in 4 consecutive at-bats in 1977.

Most Points in an NHL Game

There's nothing more exciting in a hard-fought hockey game than a goal… the red light goes on, the horn sounds, and the fans go crazy. Through the NHL's long history, some games have seen scoring shoot straight through the stratosphere. Way back in 1920, **JOE MALONE** of the Quebec Bulldogs scored 7 goals in a single game, a record that still hasn't been equaled. In the same year, Joe's Bulldogs weren't quite so lucky, as the Montreal Canadiens set the all-time record for goals scored by one team against them, striking for 16. Much later, in 1976, the Toronto Maple Leafs' **DARRYL SITTLER** scored an amazing 10 points (6 goals & 4 assists) in a single game. And if you're talking speedy, then you're talking **BILL MOSIENKO** of the Chicago Blackhawks—in 1952, he scored a hat trick (3 goals) in only 21 seconds.

Most NHL Career Penalty Minutes

Sometimes things get rough in hockey games, and the big boys come out to play. These rough and tough characters know how to lift their team and shift the momentum, whether it's through a crushing body-check or a spirited round of fisticuffs. Of course, there's usually a price to be paid, and these types of players rack up huge numbers of penalty minutes cooling their heels in the penalty box. **DAVE "TIGER" WILLIAMS,** best known as a Maple Leaf and Canuck, leads the pack with 3,966 long minutes of sin bin time. **DALE HUNTER** of the Quebec Nordiques/Washington Capitals (3,563) and **TIE DOMI** of the Leafs/Jets/Rangers (3,515) both top the 3,500-minute mark. Rounding out the top 5 are **MARTY MCSORLEY,** an Edmonton teammate of Wayne Gretzky, with 3,381, and Red Wings/Blackhawks bruiser **BOB PROBERT** with 3,300.

Source: http://www.esb.com

Most Points in NBA Finals

When the regular season is all said and done, it's time for the playoffs… and it all leads to the NBA Finals. Sometimes championships are won with tough defense, but other times it is all offense. Since the NBA Finals are a best-of-seven-games series, they can last 4 to 7 games. The total points leaders by team for each length of series are the **BOSTON CELTICS** with 487 points in 4 games (1959) and 617 points in 5 games (1965); the **PHILADELPHIA 76ERS** with 747 points in 6 games (1967); and the **CELTICS** with 827 points in 7 games (1966). The fewest points ever scored in a finals series was set by the **BALTIMORE BULLETS** in 1971, who posted only 376 points in 4 games while being swept by the **MILWAUKEE BUCKS.** But what about individual stats? The players who set the standard for individual finals scoring are **SHAQUILLE O'NEAL** of the **LOS ANGELES LAKERS** with 145 points in 4 games (2002); **ALLEN IVERSON** of the **76ERS** with 178 in 5 games (2001); **MICHAEL JORDAN** of the **CHICAGO BULLS** with 246 in 6 games (1993); and **ELGIN BAYLOR** of the **LAKERS** with 284 points in 7 games (1962).

Most Overtimes in NBA

Sometimes when the regulation time buzzer sounds, nothing has been decided… the teams are still deadlocked in a tie. In such cases, there's only one way to determine the winner—overtime, no matter how long it takes. And it can take a looooong time… just ask the 1951 **INDIANAPOLIS OLYMPIANS** and **ROCHESTER ROYALS,** who played 6 overtimes before Indy grabbed the victory. When it comes to the most overtime games in a season played by one team, no one's topped the 1991 **PHILADELPHIA 76ERS'** 14 OT games. The 2001 **SACRAMENTO KINGS** won more OT games in a season than any other team with 9. And spare a thought for the 1980 **GOLDEN STATE WARRIORS,** who were in 8 OT games that season but didn't manage to win a single one.

....Most Fumbles in NFL

Every offense in the NFL takes the field with one goal each possession… to score points. But if you want to score, you need the ball, and coughing up a fumble is a sure momentum killer. The dubious honor of handing over the pigskin most in the 2009-2010 NFL season belonged to Kansas City Chiefs quarterback **MATT CASSEL** with 9. Fellow QB **VINCE YOUNG** of the Tennesee Titans was close behind with 7 fumbles, while running back **ADRIAN PETERSON** of the Minnesota Vikings follows in third with 6. Peterson also had 2 fumbles in post-season play.

Most Points in ....an NFL Game

NFL offensive firepower can be an awesome thing when unleashed, and some scoring juggernauts over the ages have put so many points on the board that the scoreboard was in danger of overheating! The most total points in one game is 113, from a **WASHINGTON REDSKINS /NEW YORK GIANTS** clash in 1966. The 72 points scored by the **REDSKINS** in that game also stands as most by a single team. In more recent times, a **CINCINNATI BENGALS/ CLEVELAND BROWNS** game in 2004 saw Cincy post 58 points versus Cleveland's 48, good enough for the second all-time highest total of 106. On the other side of the coin, the last scoreless tie to be played in the NFL was between the **NEW YORK GIANTS** and **DETROIT LIONS** in 1943.

Ice Racing

When the weather turns cold in Minnesota and the lakes freeze up, there's only one thing to do… ice racing! The intrepid racers of the International Ice Racing Association don their cold weather gear and hurtle across an ice sheet that can range from 14 inches thick up to the **3 TO 4 FEET OF SOLID ICE** encountered in Duluth Harbor in 1989. Track lengths range from only an eighth of a mile to the long 2.3-mile tracks of LaCrosse and St. Paul. The oldest racer is Len Jackson, a 72-year-old who started his ice racing career in the late 1960s and is still going strong today. The coldest race day? A chilling minus 25 degrees at the Brainerd track in 1974.

....The Wingsuit

Not satisfied with simply falling out of airplanes, expert parachutists are now using a device called a wingsuit to allow them to fly. This looks like a regular jumpsuit with sails sewn on each side of the wearer—between the arm and leg on each side and between the legs, too. This allows the wearer to **TRAVEL FOR MILES** and extend a jump from seconds to minutes.

Largest Waves Surfed..

Using jet-skis to tow themselves into position has made it possible for surfers to ride insanely large waves. Mike Parsons holds the current record for surfing a **77-FOOT WAVE** on January 5, 2008. Later that same month, Ken Bradshaw rode a wave thought to be more than 80 feet tall, but no photographic proof of this exists.

Source: http://adventure.howstuffworks.com, http://www.surfline.com

Airboarding............➤

In the world of extreme sports, the envelope is always being pushed. The brand-new sport known as airboarding does just that, and has rapidly expanded across the globe. Airboards are inflated sleds with a triangular tip that allows carving. Riders go down snow-covered slopes face-first on the sleds while holding on to handles and maneuvering, tricking, and catching big air! Typical speeds are in the 60 mph range, but the current speed record is held by Switzerland's Laurent Matthey, who hit **88.1 MPH** in Les Arcs, France.

Rowing Across The Atlantic
Longest Distance Rowed In 1 Day

When a record stands for 114 years, you know it is hard to break. But that is exactly what Leven Brown, Livar Nysted, Don Lennox, and Ray Carroll did when they smashed the speed record for rowing across the Atlantic Ocean by 11 days. Braving high seas and multiple equipment failure, the four men took **43 DAYS, 21 HOURS, 26 MINUTES, AND 48 SECONDS** to row from New York to England's Isles of Scilly in their 23-foot boat, *Artemis Investments*. The 2-man crew whose record they beat, George Harbo and Frank Samuelsen, were promised a $10,000 reward for the feat in 1896, but it was never delivered.

As part of the all-time-fastest Atlantic crossing by rowboat, the Artemis Investments team also established the mark for the longest distance rowed in a single day. July 14, 2010, saw the four-man team row an astounding **118 MILES**—a distance equal to a trip from Manhattan to the tip of Long Island. This remarkable performance shaved a whole day off the previous record, set in 2008. On other days of their journey, the team had to deal with a crew-wide bout of food poisoning, as well as an emergency toe surgery performed with a knife!

Source: http://www.airboarders.com, http://www.deccanherald.com, http://www.oceanrowevents.com

Mega Mountainboard Track

The Nate Harrison Grade is a legendary spot for mountain biking and mountainboarding just outside of San Diego, CA. Located on the side of Palomar Mountain, the climbing portion is a major challenge on a mountain bike, rising 4,700 feet from the starting point. And the downhill is mountainboard heaven... **7 MILES OF SERIOUSLY FAST TERRAIN.** The Nate Harrison Grade Downhill Race is held there each year, with the current titleholder Kody Stewart completing the track in a blazing 19 minutes and 17 seconds, more than a minute faster than the second-place finisher. In the Youth division, 9-year-old Damien Hertenstein finished first with a time of 38 minutes and 30 seconds.

UNBREAKABLE

Best Athlete of the 20th Century

The argument over who was the greatest athlete of the 20th century will probably continue until the end of the 21st. Strong cases can be made for Muhammed Ali, Michael Jordan, Wayne Gretzky, and Pelé, but perhaps none of them can top the credentials of **JIM THORPE.** A descendent of the great Sac and Fox Chief Black Hawk, Thorpe became a football All-American under legendary coach Pop Warner. He went on to 1912 Olympic gold medals in pentathalon and decathalon. Next up for Thorpe was Major League Baseball, where he played six seasons with four teams. At the same time, Thorpe was also playing professional football. He drew huge crowds as a Canton Bulldog, an early foobtall powerhouse, and also had a stint as player-coach of the all-Native American team the Oorang Indians. Jim Thorpe retired in 1928 and died in 1953, leaving behind a legacy that will never be equalled.

Ultra Weight Throw

Based on track and field's hammer throw, a weight throw is performed within a 7-foot circular boundary and utilizes a two-handed toss. But whereas a hammer weighs 16 pounds, ultra weight throwers are in another universe entirely—they hurl weights of **98, 200, AND 300 POUNDS!** The men's record for both 98 (19' 11") and 300 pounds (6' 1/4") is held by Jim Wetenhall, while Paul Brown has the title at 200 pounds (10' 1 1/4"). Although no woman has made a 300-pound toss, Vanessa Hilliard is best at 98 pounds (10' 1 1/4", the same distance as men's 200-lb.) and Sara Buslaugh is tops at 200 pounds (2' 5").

Source: http://www.mountainbikebill.com, Strength & Speed by Dale Harder, http://www.cmgww.com

Worldwide Marathons

A guy who's had a heart attack and a double-bypass operation isn't the first person you'd think of when imagining a **GLOBE-TROTTING MARATHONER.** But Dr. Michael Stroud of Great Britain can certainly claim that title. Between October 26 and November 2 of 2003, he and his friend Sir Ranulph Fiennes competed in consecutive marathons in Santiago, Chile; the Falkland Islands; Sydney, Australia; Singapore; London, England; and New York City.

UNBREAKABLE

Marathon of the Sands

Of all the footraces held around the world, one has to be the absolute toughest—and there's no doubt it's the **MARATHON DES SABLES (MARATHON OF THE SANDS),** held yearly in Morocco. This brutal test of superhuman endurance is run over 151 miles of the toughest terrain the Sahara Desert can dish out: shifting sands, razor-sharp rock plains, and dried lake beds. Runners must carry their own water, medicine, food, and tents over the six-day event, whose distance is equal to five-and-a-half marathons. Daytime temperatures can rise to 1▮▮ degrees before plummeting into the 40s at night, and runners are advised to wear shoes a size and a half too big to accomodate for severe swelling.

Swinging 360s

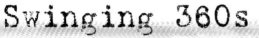

Swinging is a tradition in Estonia, with 4-person wooden swings used at festivals a common site in villages even today. This evolved into the sport of kiiking (pronounced "keeking," from *kiik*, Estonian for "swing") in 1996, with the first modern telescopic-frame kiiking swing. Similar to high jump, the competitors name a height (measured from the swing's flat base), which then must be reached by "clearing the spindle"... that is, **A 360 ON THE SWING!** Although each competitor has five tries, only three are usually used because of the strenuousness of the activity. Five minutes are given to clear the bar, but competitors can rarely do more than three minutes on the swing. The sport has spread to Finland, Sweden, and Belarus, so who knows—maybe there will be a swing in your town soon, too.

Source: Strength & Speed by Dale Harder, http://www.kiiking.ee

Fastest Men And Women On Bikes

Elite athletes can hit remarkable speeds on bicycles, such as Sam Whittingham, the world's fastest cyclist, who reached a **TOP SPEED OF 82.8 MPH.** France's Barbara Buatois is the world's fastest woman cyclist, having hit 75.7 mph. The fastest time to cover 100 miles by a man is 2 hours 11 minutes by Alex Fehlau, and the woman's record of 2 hours 43 minutes is held by Ellen van Vugt. Both 100-mile records were set on the Opel Proving Grounds, and all four records were set on a flat track using recumbent (seated) bicycles with an aerodynamic shell, known as human powered vehicles (HPVs).

Longest Rides

Chris Boardman holds the record for the furthest distance ridden on an ordinary bicycle in one hour with a mark of 35 miles; he therefore maintained an incredible average speed of 35 mph! The one-hour record on an HPV set by Sam Whittingham is 56.3 miles, while Barbara Buatois went 52.2 miles. Alex Fehlau claims the title in six hours, averaging 44.2 mph to cover 265 miles, while Ellen van Vugt averaged 35 mph to cover 210 miles. Christian Ascheberg set the record for a full 24-hour period with **A DISTANCE OF 760 MILES**—more than the driving distance from San Francisco to Salt Lake City—using a streamlined recumbent racing tricycle.

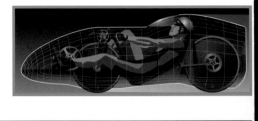

NEWS YOU CAN USE
STREND

For a real test of fitness, it's hard to beat the Strend events. Strend, which **STANDS FOR "STRENGTH" AND "ENDURANCE,"** is a group of 6 events in which competitors push themselves to the limit. It's also an excellent program for training at home, and the weights utilized in the strength events are customized to each person's bodyweight. The 6 events are: Pull-ups; Chin-ups; Bench Pressing your bodyweight; Seated behind-the-neck press (bodyweight); Parallel Bar dips; and a 3-mile run. For all but the run, the athlete has 3 minutes to perform the maximum reps possible.

Source: http://www.ihpva.org, Strength & Speed by Dale Harder

NEWS YOU CAN USE

How to Toss a Caber

A highlight of any Scottish games is the caber toss—the throwing of a 15- to 20-foot-long log, or caber, which can weigh **UP TO 190 POUNDS**. The object is to get the caber to go end-over-end and land as straight as possible, although if it doesn't flip completely over it is scored on how close it got. Once you've trained hard and got your hands on a caber, you're ready to toss: 1) Stand the caber on its end... help is permitted!; 2) Pick the caber up, using hands with fingers interlaced; 3) With your hands underneath the end of the caber, balance it on your shoulder; 4) Start walking or running with the caber; 5) Toss that caber! Stop quickly, bend your legs, and heave the caber up and out, attempting to get the end you were holding up and over the top. Now catch your breath and take a rest!

Iron Stomach... ▶

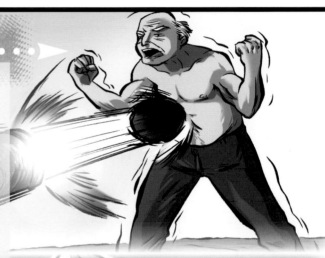

1920s carnival performer Frank Richards may have had the strongest abdomen of all time. He trained himself over the years to withstand blows to the gut that would certainly injure, if not kill, a normal person... and never stopped trying to top his last feat. First Frank challenged the then-current heavyweight champion Jack Dempsey to punch him in the abodmen... which Dempsey did, 75 times! Unfazed, Richards moved on to taking blows from 4x4 boards wielded like baseball bats (which were too puny to be bothered with). Next came sledgehammer strikes, but it still wasn't enough. Richards settled on the act that would be his most popular... standing 6 feet in front of a 12-foot-long cannon and taking the **104-POUND CANNONBALL SHOT STRAIGHT IN THE STOMACH.** He would sometimes be knocked to the ground by the force of the shot, but would remain totally unhurt.

.... Don't Smash Your Face

Hammer levering is pretty much the definition of a "don't try this at home" sport, as the consequences of a mishap are gruesome to contemplate. It's accomplished by taking a sledgehammer (average weight around 25 pounds) and holding it in one hand. The hammer is lifted or swung with one hand until it is above the head and the arm holding it is straight out from the body. Then comes the really hard part—the hammer is lowered slowly, using only the hand holding it, straight toward the face! Once the **HEAD OF THE HAMMER TOUCHES THE NOSE**, it is raised back to an upright position and the task is complete.

Source: Strength & Speed by Dale Harder

WHO'S GOT NEXT?

Orangutan Hang

Some athletic feats require speed to master, some raw strength. But others are accomplished by pure **ENDURANCE AND RESISTANCE TO PAIN.** Definitely falling into the last category is the one-armed hang, commonly known as the Orangutan Hang. While simple in theory—hang from a bar with one hand without touching the ground for as long as possible—it is devilishly hard to accomplish for any length of time. The current record holder, Matt Bogdanowicz, hung by his left arm for 1 minute and 45 seconds, while managing a 1:37 hang with his right. That may not seem like a long time, but it is an eternity to the person attempting it.

Human Cannonballs

In the past, the human cannonball was always a crowd-pleasing stunt, with crowds roaring in approval as daredevils were expelled from cannons and soared up to 100 feet in the air and 200 feet in length. The stunt was invented by a performer known as the Great Farini in 1877, when a 14-year-old girl named Zazel was propelled 30 feet into a net. Human cannonballs are not actually shot like a real cannonball— rather, an explosion is timed to go off at the same time that a spring-loaded platform pushes the person out of the barrel, simulating a shot. Perhaps the reason that we don't see this stunt much these days is that two-thirds of the performers that attempted the stunt were **KILLED WHEN THEY MISSED THE NET.**

Ex-Olympic Sports

When athletes gather every four years for the Olympic Games, the world watches and is exposed to many new and unfamiliar sports. Over the years, many sports have either been tried as a demonstration but not added to the Games, or simply dropped. For instance, do you know that lacrosse, golf, and rugby were once Olympic sports? Some of the stranger discontinued events were the rope climb, an **UNDERWATER SWIMMING RACE,** nation vs. nation tug of war, and even a live pigeon-shooting contest.

Source: Strength & Speed by Dale Harder, http://www.topendsports.com

...Breathtaking Sports

Sports rely on all sorts of special talents... but breath control? Two unusual sports rely on just that. The ping pong variant blo-ball features a net-less table with adjustable legs. The table is adjusted to the height of the players, who use their breath to **PROPEL A PING PONG BALL** back and forth while attempting to get it to go off their opponent's side of the table. In the Indian sport kabaddi, two teams take turns sending a raider into their opponents territory, where he tries to tag as many opposing players as possible. The time limit for the raider is determined by how long he can hold his breath, which he must demonstrate by chanting "kabaddi" the entire time he is tagging.

Super Strange Sports

The need to compete is built into humankind. What some people consider strange activites, others call sport, and give their all to come out on top. Consider the Cooper Hill cheese rolling competition in Gloucester, England, where the aim is to **ROLL A 7-POUND CHEESE WHEEL** down the steep grade while keeping pace behind it. England is also home to toe wrestling, an arm wrestling variant staged in a "toedium" and where a competitor can quit by yelling "toe much"! Not limited by geography at all is extreme ironing, where competitors try to top each other by ironing in the most outrageous places possible... such as the tops of mountains, under waterfalls, on top of cars, or while bungee jumping!

Off to the Races

People all over the world love a race... and love to speculate beforehand who will come out on top! Whether for a big payday or purely for the joy of sport, races have been staged with an amazing array of animals. In the Middle East you will find camel races, complete with robotic "jockeys." In the Caribbean, **CRABS WITH NUMBERS PAINTED ON THEIR BACKS** compete to see which is fastest. Best represented of all is Australia, where the old saying is that people will bet on flies racing up the wall. Although no documented fly races can be found, the land down under does stage races between cane toads, cockroaches, cows, lizards, pigs, sheep, and yabbies (crayfish).

YOUTH SPORTS

WHO'S GOT NEXT?

GO FOR IT!

The pros get all the press, but if you think that kids don't set their own amazing sports records then you haven't been paying attention! All the records in this section were set by athletes of high school age or younger, and they are all ripe for the taking. If you, or an athlete from your school, break one of these records (or another amazing sporting record), we want to hear about it! See the last page of this chapter for details on how you can submit the record for inclusion in next year's Book of Extreme Facts.

Home Run Heroics

The long home run ball is arguably the most exciting play in baseball, and it's no different in the high school ranks. The career leader for high school home runs is **JEFF CLEMENT,** currently with the Pittsburgh Pirates, who hit 75 in his tenure at Marshalltown, IA. Eight-year Major Leaguer **WADE MILLER** set the single season record in his high school days in Alabama with 30. The single game record for homers is 5, with 5 players sharing the honors. The career high school record holder for Grand Slams is Brighton, MI's **DREW HENSON,** who later played not only Major League Baseball but NFL football as well!

Baseball Offensive Powerhouses

If you like high-powered scoring, high school baseball is the sport for you. This was especially true in the past, with **TUCSON, AZ's** high school team averaging 16.7 runs per game way back in 1935. Eight years earlier, the biggest blowout in high school baseball occurred, with **ATLANTIC, IA,** beating Griswold, IA, by a score of 109 to nothing! In more recent times, **BELMONT, MS,** set the record in 1999 for most runs all-time in one inning with 37.

Softball Sensations

Twice in history, in 1983 and 2001, a girls' high school softball game has gone an exhausting 35 innings to complete… both times in California. Lousiana is home to the two schools with the longest consecutive win streaks: **VANDERBILT CATHOLIC** with 112 wins in a row and **LAKE CHARLES BARBE** with 107. Barbe was also the team of **CANDICE CARNAHAN,** who hurled 50 no-hitters over the course of her career. In the batter's box, **JANET WEISENFORTH** of Green Island Heatly, NY, hit 5 home runs in a single game. In 2002, **AUBREY MARTIN** of Muscatine, IA, hit two grand slams in a single inning, tying her with 3 others who had also accomplished the remarkable feat.

Girls Basketball Legends

No girl ever scored more over a high school career than **ADRIAN MCGOWEN** of Goodrich, TX, with 5,424 points. **GERI GRIGSBY** of McDowell, KY, was no slouch in the mid-1970s, though—she still holds the all-time season (1,885 points) and career per-game average (46.1 points per game) records. Circleville, WV's **CHRISTY COOPER** averaged 60 points per game during the 1988-1989 season, but ranks four spots lower than Grigsby on the career average list. There have been two 100+ point performances in girls' basketball history: **CHERYL MILLER'S** 105 in 1982 and **LISA LESLIE'S** 101 in 1990. Leslie's record is more remarkable, as she scored all 101 points in the first half before refusing to take the court for the second half.

Boys Hoops Phenoms

Lousiana legend **GREG PROCELL'S** 6,702 career point record has stood since 1970… with 3,173 of those points coming in his senior season. In fact, number two all-time career scorer Bruce Williams is second by 1,335 points! The boys' game has seen 15 players score 100 or more points in a single game, with Burnsville, WV's **DANNY HEATER** setting the standard with 135 points in 1960. Portland Trailblazer legend **BILL WALTON** is the most accurate field goal shooter over the course of the season, sinking 78.3 of his attempts for San Diego's Helix High in 1969-1970. **TAUREAN MOY** of Memphis Booker T. Washington represents the long-range bombers, sinking 24 three-pointers (from 44 attempts) in 2000.

Source: http://www.nfhs.org

They Never Lose

In high school football, there are win streaks, and then there is "The Streak" set by **DE LA SALLE H.S.** in Concord, CA. After winning the opening game of the 1992 season, the Spartans went on to win the following 150 games, with their streak ending at 151 on opening day of the 2004 season, with a loss to Bellevue High School. This mark destroyed the old record of 72 straight wins. In fact, their coach **BOB LADOUCEUR** has lost only 22 games at De La Salle since beginning his career in 1979.

Touchdown!

Football is all about getting into that end zone… just ask **MICHAEL HART** of Nedrow Onondaga, NY, whose 2000-2003 career included a high school record 204 TDs. **T.A. MCLENDON** of Albermarle, NC, holds the mark for most TDs in a season, scoring 71 of them in 2001. The most amazing TD performance in a game—13 touchdowns—is held by two players separated by 40 years: **RICKY LANIER** of Williamstown Hayes, NC, did it in 1967, while **ELVIN MCCOY** of Haven, KS, set the mark way back in 1927.

Superfeet

Mentally, the kicker has one of the toughest positions on a football team. They are called on only a few times a game, but are expected to be perfect every time. Mental toughness like that is rare in a high schooler, but **KIM BRASWELL** of Avondale Estates, GA, had ice in his veins in kicking 134 consecutive extra points in the late 1960s. When it comes to field goals, Albuquerque, NM's **DOMINIC GUTIERREZ** holds the most-in-a-game record with 9. **DIRK BORGOGNONE** of Reno, NV, holds the distance record, kicking a 68-yarder in 1985 that has yet to be equaled or beat.

Rocket Arms

The quarterback is the unquestioned leader of a football team, and the high school ranks have witnessed many a legendary performance by young QBs. In 2000, **DAVID KORAL** of Pacific Palisades, CA, set a single-game passing record by hurling for 764 yards! The highest passing-yards-per-game mark (436 yards) is held by **BEN MAUK** of Kenton, OH, whose career 17,364 passing yards is also the best ever. Ten touchdown passes thrown in a single game is a record shared by 5 players, one of whom is David Koral.

Rink Rulers

Just as De La Salle is unquestionably the best high school football team, **MT. SAINT CHARLES ACADEMY** of Woonsocket, RI, stands head and shoulders above the competition in high school ice hockey. The Mounties are ahead by a mile in a host of record categories, including a 5-year winning streak of 94 consecutive victories. Even more astounding is their state champion trophy case, which includes 40 state championships. Twenty-six of those 40 championships were consecutive, as no other team could claim the title between 1978 and 2003.

Elite Receivers

Even the best pass is only successful if it is caught, and a receiver's performance after the catch can often break a football game wide open. Los Angeles Cathedral's **EARVIN JOHNSON** set the single game TD mark in 1998, hauling down 8 touchdown passes. More recently, **J.D. FELICE** of Rose Bud, AR, set the one-game receiving yardage mark in 2008 with 421 yards. However, the record for most total receptions in one game is one of the longest lasting: **LARRY BENNETT** of Mogadore, OH, caught 32 passes against Ohio rival Hudson way back in 1942.

Source: http://www.nfhs.org

Kings of the Ice

Besides New England, the Midwest is the United States' other high school hockey hotbed. This area produced **JIM JOHNSON,** whose 1971-1974 career at Bloomfield Hills Cranbrook-Kingswood, in Michigan, resulted in a record 249 goals scored, 20 ahead of runner-up Casey Kutner of New Jersey. Michiganders **RON ROLSTON** (in '84) and **CRAIG HUMPHREY** (in '90) share the record for scoring 10 goals in one game, while Scott Long dished out a record 11 assists for Mt. Morris in 1994. Wisconsin is represented in goal, with **GLENN WALKER** of Verona stopping 48 shots for the most-saves record in 2003.

Ladies First

With the U.S. soccer explosion in full swing for twenty years now, high schoolers everywhere are setting incredible marks on the pitch. **JENNIER BRELAGE** of Bardstown, KY, hit the back of the net 18 times in one game in 2002, a girls' high school record. Almost as good was **MELISSA WELLS** of New Port Richey, FL, who scored 14 times in a 1991 game. The girls' career assist leader is North Carolinian **LEIGH MURRAY,** who dished out 153 over 4 seasons at Kernersville East. Not surprisingly, Leigh Murray is also the single-game assist leader, setting up teammates 10 times against Winton-Salem Carver in 1989.

She Saves!

Soccer games are usually low-scoring affairs, thanks to the skills of the goalkeeper. Nothing is more sought after in net than the "clean sheet"… posting a shutout by preventing the opponent from getting any goals. Boca Raton, FL's **KATHRYN KNECHT** has a career-best 72 shutouts, while **KELLY BERKEMEIER** of St. Mary's in Stockton, CA, has the single-season shutout record of 32. Perhaps most remarkable of all is the consecutive shutout record of 21 in a row, established in 2001 by **AMY PRICE** of Omaha, NE´s Marian H.S.

Goals and Hat Tricks

U.S. boys' soccer boasts some incredible goal scoring records, like **SEAN SHAPERT'S** 213 career goals and **MICHAEL RICHARDSON'S** 92 goals in a season. Almost beyond belief are performances like **DALE SELF** of Sumter, SC's 14-goal performance in 2002 or **JOSE TAMAYO** of Greenfield, CA's 12-assist game a year earlier. Then there is the hat trick record, commemorating a 3-goal performance by a single player. Jeremy Hardy of Cooks, MI, had a 6-game hat trick streak going TWICE, but that is still not good enough for top spot. **JAMISON IMHOFF** of New Covenant Christian in Lansing, MI, went an astounding 9 games in a row scoring a hat trick in 2008.

Speed Demons

While records are important in all sports, they perhaps mean most of all in track. These athletes may line up next to others, but the clock is their main opponent. The fastest boys' high school 400-meter dash time is held by **CALVIN HARRISON** of North Salinas, CA, who ran it in 45.25 seconds in 1993. **ROY MARTIN** of Dallas' Roosevelt High School is fastest at 200 meters with 20.13 seconds, which beat his own previous record. The jewel of track is the 100-meter dash, and this high school record was set in 1990 by **HENRY NEAL** of Greenville, TX, who crushed Roy Martin's previous record with a blazing time of 10.15 seconds.

Mighty Minders

Even though boys' high school soccer tends to feature more scoring than higher levels, a goalkeeper that was forced to make 30 saves in a game would think he had a very busy day indeed. Imagine the two keepers that have made more than 50 saves in a single game—**DAVID WELL** of St. Teresa, IL, with 52 and **MIKE SIMONE** of Sanborn, NH, with 51. When it comes to hot streaks, a goalkeeper on a consecutive shutout roll is frightening indeed. Three high school goalkeepers—**TYLER FITCH, CHRISTOPHER NECKLAS, AND BRETT SCHAEFER**—share the record of 16 consecutive shutouts, with Necklas and Schaefer doing it in 2002 and Fitch equaling the record in 2008.

Source: http://www.nfhs.org

Hopping and Hurling

Field events test the strength, power, and leaping ability of boys' high school competitors. The long jump standard of 26 feet 4 3/4 inches set by Tulare, CA's **JAMES STALLWORTH** has stood since 1989. The record Stallworth beat had been set in 1972, which shows how hard this record is to break. 2009 saw **JAMES WHITE** of Grandview, MO, tie **DOTHEL EDWARDS** of Athens, GA, with a high jump of 7 feet 5 3/4 inches. That's like jumping over Lebron James with 9 inches to spare! For an amazing feat of strength, consider **MICHAEL CARTER** of Dallas, TX's 77-foot shot put toss in 1979. The metal ball used in high school shot put weighs twelve pounds!

Best Girls H.S. Track

There must be something in the water out there, because Southern California is home to the girls' 400-, 200-, and 100-meter dash record holders. San Diego's F.B. Morse H.S. produced **MONIQUE HENDERSON,** who ran the 400 in 50.74 seconds in 2000. Los Angeles Baptist was represented by **ALLYSON FELIX** in the 200 when she set the current mark at 22.52 seconds. And Thousand Oaks' **MARION JONES,** who went on to star in the Summer Games in Sydney and the WNBA, still holds the 100-meter dash record she set in 1992 when she ran it in 11.14 seconds.

Best Girls H.S. Field

Just as on the boys' side, the girls' high school long jump record has proven to be an incredibly hard one to break. While records fell in quick succession for four years in a row in the early '70s, the mark has remained at 22 feet 1 3/4 inches set by **KATHY MCMILLAN** of Raeford Hoke County, NC, since 1976. Oakhurst, CA's **ANASTASIA JELMINI** is the high school record discus hurler, tossing the 1 kg (2 lb. 3 oz.) disc 190.3 feet, or over 63 yards! The girls shot put weighs 8 pounds, and in 2003 **MICHELLE CARTER** of Red Oak, TX, broke a 20-year-old record with a throw of 54 feet 10 3/4 inches.

Lax's Powell Power

The ranks of high school lacrosse have never seen a family like the amazing Powell brothers. **CASEY, RYAN, AND MIKE POWELL** (from oldest to youngest) call a huge chunk of the lacrosse record book their own. Casey holds the most career goals record with 292, while Ryan is second (244 goals), and Mike is fifth (200). Casey is also tops with 553 career points, with Mike second (499) and Ryan fourth (429). Mike claims top spot in most assists in a season (120) and most points in a single season (194). Not to be denied a #1 slot, Ryan claimed the record for most assists in a game with 11. And the accolades listed here are only a small part of the long line of record performances turned in by the brothers from Carthage, NY.

Volleyballin'

Girls' volleyball has traditionally drawn some of the best high-school-age female athletes in the nation, but teamwork is the key to winning. **SAFFORD, AZ,** holds the consecutive state championship record with 21 in a row, followed closely by Muncie Burris, IN's 20 straight. Individually, **ALISHA GLASS** of Leland, MI, is the standard setter. She holds the career (937) and season (296) records for service aces, or serving a ball that is not returned by the other team. The record for career kills—spikes that are not returned and result in a point—is also owned by Alisha with 3,584. She's no slacker on defense either, as her 680 career blocks are best in high school history.

Mat Legends

If all you know about wrestling is the pro pay-for-view stuff, then you don't know the sport. The real thing is practiced in high schools across the nation, drawing remarkable athletes to test their strength and agility against one another. **PERRY H.S.** of Oklahoma has taken home the most team titles in the nation, with 37 state titles since 1952. When it comes to career victories, **TRAVIS SULLIVAN** of Monticello, KY's Wayne County H.S. is tops with 304, but **JUSTIN ZEERIP** of Hesperia, MI, is tops in consecutive victories, reeling off 260 in a row. Zeerip is also the owner of the record for career falls—when a wrestler pins their opponent—with 203. If you're wondering about the fastest fall, there are a host of records depending on weight class, but so far 3 seconds is the fastest it's ever been done.

Source: http://www.nfhs.org

Best Little Leaguer Ever

Hailing from Hamtramck, MI, **ART "PINKY" DERAS** may well be the best little league pitcher ever. The sheer volume of games worldwide prevent exact statistics, but Deras' numbers in 1959 are mind-boggling. Of his 18 victories that year (all of which were complete games), 16 of them were shutouts. Deras was not content to keep the opponents off the board, however, hurling five straight no-hitters and ten total for the season. He threw 75 straight scoreless innings as his team marched to a shutout in the 1959 Little League World Series final. As a batter, Deras contributed 112 RBIs and 33 homers that season, further solidifying his claim to the title of greatest of all time.

Longest Snowball Throw

When winter rolls around and snow comes down, it's time for snowballs. Everyone who's lived in the white stuff has chucked one, but some people are able to heave them a lot farther than others. At Oslo's Bislett Games of track and field, kids compete using snowballs that weigh around 14 ounces made with a commercial machine. Locals **MARKUS JOHANSEN** and **KRISTINA KRISTIANSLUND** hold the current records, with throws of 230' 11" and 197' 6", respectively. Now that is long-range bombing!

GET IN THE ACTION!

Why just read the **BOOK OF EXTREME FACTS** when you can be featured in it yourself? Perhaps this chapter has inspired you to set or share some records of your own, such as:

• Amazing elementary school sports feats!
• High school sports heroics!
• Fantastic feats of athletic prowess!

Remember, you are not limited to the above suggestions, or to trying to beat other records in this chapter. Entirely new records are not only allowed... they are encouraged! The only limit is your own creativity. So have some fun (but always remember to keep it SAFE), and if you are younger than 18 remember to ask your parents for permission before attempting any record.

To submit a record:

-Go to *www.bookofextremefacts.com*

-Click on the "Submit New Record" tab

-Provide a brief description of your record and your contact info

-If we decide that your record makes the grade, we will contact you for further details and photos or video of your record

It's just that simple! Good luck...
and **KEEP IT EXTREME!**

Involvement in dangerous sports and related activities carries a significant risk of damage to property, personal injury, or death. Please do not endanger yourself or others or take any unnecessary risks. If you choose to participate in dangerous sports or activities in attempting to achieve a distinction that would be recognized in the next edition of the Book of Extreme Facts, which IDW does not recommend, you do so at your own risk. IDW suggests the use of professional instruction before entering into any sports or physical activity. You should become knowledgeable about the risks involved. By submitting information to IDW related to inclusion in a future edition of the Book of Extreme Facts you assume personal responsibility for your actions and agree to indemnify and hold harmless IDW for the consequences of your actions.

IMAGE CREDITS

Page 6 - MOST SUCCESSFUL WINDSURFER
      Photo by Martin Haglev
Page 7 - INDIVIDUAL 3-3-3 & 3-6-3 SPORT STACKING
      Photo by Larry Goers, Speed Stacks, Inc.
Page 7 - TIMED 3-6-3 RELAY STACKING
      Photo by Larry Goers, Speed Stacks, Inc.
Page 7 - WOMEN'S OUTDOOR BOOT THROWING
      Photo by Pasi Kuusinen
Page 7 - MEN'S OUTDOOR BOOT THROWING
      Photo by Pasi Kuusinen
Page 8 - MOST WORLD SERIES HOME RUNS MICKEY MANTLE
      Photo by Tony the Misfit
Page 8 - MOST WORLD SERIES HOME RUNS REGGIE JACKSON
      Photo by Googie man
Page 10 - ICE RACING Photo by Royalbroil
Page 13 - WORLDWILD MARATHON Photo by Martineric
Page 13 - MARATHON OF THE SANDS Photo by James Heilman, MD
Page 16 - EX-OLYMPIC SPORTS Photo by adrian8_8
Page 17 - SUPER STRANGE SPORTS Photo by BrianP

CHAPTER 2
EXTREME RECORDS

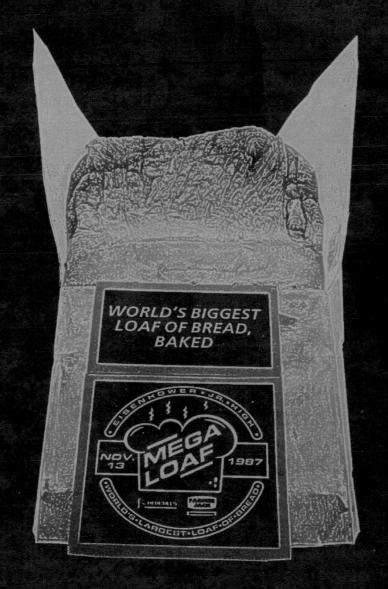

WORLD'S BIGGEST LOAF OF BREAD, BAKED

WHO'S GOT NEXT?

GO FOR IT!

The Extreme Records chapter of the **BOOK OF EXTREME FACTS 2012** is **your chance** to get into the action. You'll notice that this chapter features multiple records set by a few dedicated record seekers, like **Eisenhower Junior High School**, **Mick Cullen**, and **Brian Pankey**. While all these record breakers will no doubt continue to achieve new feats, we hope their records will inspire **you** to get involved in some record-breaking events of your own. The final page of each chapter of this book has complete information on how to get involved.

Largest Stick-On Note Mosaic

Stick-on notes are great for marking book pages and leaving reminders, but making a mosaic? How about one measuring **60 x 40 FEET?!** That's exactly what Eisenhower Junior High School students in Taylorsville, UT, created on November 6, 2009. The massive mosaic took the labors of 151 students, who worked on the piece for 3 hours. In that time they laid down an incredible 38,400 stick-on notes of different colors, forming their school initials, the phrase "Go Green," and various designs. The notes were recycled after use.

Fastest Human Conveyer Belt

On March 3, 2005, 100 students from Eisenhower Junior High laid down side by side on the floor, feet tucked together and hands on their stomachs. Their mission: using only the rolling of their bodies, the students would seek to act as a human conveyer belt to move a mattress from one end to the other. When it was all over, the students had moved the 11.4 pound mattress swiftly down the line, achieving a distance of **JUST UNDER 180 FEET** in an elapsed time of **TWO MINUTES AND ONE SECOND.**

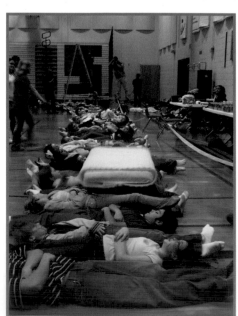

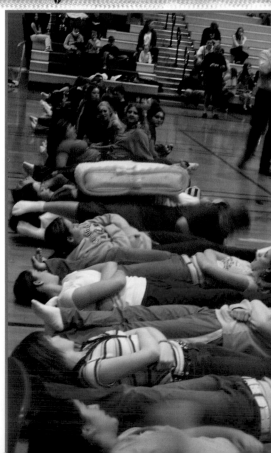

Source: http://www.claytonbrough.org/worldrecordsforschools.html

Tallest Ice Cream Cone

After a close but failed attempt on March 21, 2005, a 3-person team of Eisenhower Junior High students managed to set the record for the world's tallest ice cream cone on May 16 of the same year. The titanic treat rose to a drippy height of **13 INCHES TALL.** The cone must be constructed to rigorous standards: 3-member teams with a scooper, cone holder, and scoop placer; a 20-minute time limit; no touching of the ice cream except with scoopers or spoons (drips are an exception!); limitations on cone and base scoop width; and strict requirements for the state of the room and the ice cream when the attempt is made.

UNBREAKABLE

Largest Loaf of Bread

Eisenhower Junior High School's first-ever attempt at a world record took place way back in 1987... and that record still stands today. The combined forces of the school's industrial arts, home ec, and science departments managed to produce a huge loaf of bread measuring **7' LONG x 2.5' WIDE x 1.8' TALL.** This leviathan of a loaf weighed in at **307 LBS.** The part that makes this record tough to beat is the oven that was needed to bake it—a huge autoclave oven used to make casings for solid-fuel rocket booster motors!

WORLD'S BIGGEST LOAF OF BREAD, BAKED

EISENHOWER · JR · HIGH
MEGA LOAF
NOV. 13 1987
WORLD'S · LARGEST · LOAF · OF · BREAD

Source: http://www.claytonbrough.org/worldrecordsforschools.html

Mega Chain

What can sixty 9th graders accomplish in just twenty-four hours? They can create Mega Chain, as Eisenhower Junior High students did in March 2004. Working in teams and taking shifts to rest, the students linked **1,560,377 PAPER CLIPS** together end to end. As the chain grew, it was wrapped around a square wooden framework specially constructed for the task, which took up most of the school gym. The result was a continuous chain reaching the absolutely incredible length of **22.17 MILES!**

Longest Balloon Chain

Building on their success with the Mega Chain, the kids of Eisenhower Junior High School, along with two adults, decided to tackle making a chain of another sort—balloons! Their quest was to make the longest balloon chain they possibly could within a one-hour time limit. The 20-person construction team split up the duties of inflating the balloons and assembling the chain. When the hour had elapsed, over **1,200 BALLOONS** had been used to create a ballon chain just over **708 FEET** long.

Source: http://www.claytonbrough.org/worldrecordsforschools.html

..555 Mariachis

The 28th annual La Frontera Tucson International Mariachi Conference, held in May 2010, unleashed a mariachi band on the world unlike any that had come before. The band was made up of students, instructors, and professional mariachis from across the Southwest. They dressed in traditional mariachi garb, used traditional instruments, and played songs from Jalisco, birthplace of the style. But far from a normal line-up of a handful of mariachis, this mind-blowing band consisted of **555 PEOPLE!**

Mega Straw

Eisenhower Junior High students, not content with building massive paperclip and balloon chains, decided to give the "mega" treatment to a drinking straw chain. 33 students gathered after school and began a job that would last 8 full hours. The completed chain, constructed entirely of straight and bendable straws, reached a length of **4.57 MILES**—that's 24,166' 9"! If you try to beat that, you better bring a lot of straws—the EJHS team used **42,962** of them.

World's Tallest Pencil Tower

Constructing a pencil tower is a difficult task requiring a lot of careful planning and an extremely steady hand. The pencils used must be completely standard, with no notches or any other alterations permitted that would make them easier to stack. Record-setting Eishenhower Junior High set the mark in this category twice, first in 2005 with a 7' 2" tower, then again the following year with a 9' 6" tower. But the current record holder is Missouri's Trenton High School. Over a three-day period in 2007, students there used **1,308 PENCILS** to create a pencil tower standing **12 FEET HIGH!**

Source: http://www.yumasun.com, http://www.claytonbrough.org/worldrecordsforschools.html

Quite a Mouthful

So you think your name is kind of ho-hum, or too long to fit on forms? You've got no problems compared to the former George Garratt from Glastonbury, UK. Now 21, the youth decided to make a big splash by legally changing his name to the longest one he could think of. Now if you see him, don't call him George... use his new name: **CAPTAIN FANTASTIC FASTER THAN SUPERMAN SPIDERMAN BATMAN WOLVERINE HULK AND THE FLASH COMBINED.**

Massive Cupcake Tower

When the Gulf High School Interact club sets out to make an impression, they do it in a big way! To publicize their efforts in helping the American Cancer Society, the students came up with the 10,000 Cupcake Challenge. They built a massive, 10-foot-high tower to house the cupcakes and set out seeking donations. After 7,000 cupcakes were procured in the first 3 days, their goal looked secure, but then the cupcakes slowed to a trickle. But that trickle turned into a flood in the last days of their cupcake drive, and when the cupcake tower was completed, it contained a whopping **13,476 CUPCAKES!**

Source: http://www.independent.co.uk, http://suncoastpasco.tbo.com

Young Foosball Master

No matter what you call it—table soccer, foosball, or *futbolin*—it's fun! While just whacking away at the ball is enjoyable, getting the knack for scoring goals can be hard, especially for younger players. Xavier Cullen, though, shows an early mastery of the game and owns a world record to prove it. Xavier scored **19 GOALS IN A ONE-MINUTE TIME SPAN** to set the mark for seven-year-olds. The record must be performed completely solo, using the same ball for each attempt and taking each shot from the table's penalty kick area.

Follow the Bouncing Ball

Mick Cullen of Lindenhurst, IL, is the father of two record-holding sons. They were first inspired by Mick's own feats, of which there are many. An area of special interest for Mick is table tennis. He honed his talents over many long hours, building a skill set that necessarily includes dexterity, concentration, and tolerance for tedium. Using conventional paddles, Mick set records for most consecutive bounces on alternating sides of a single paddle **(2,256)** and alternating sides of two paddles **(1,692)**. Using not-so-conventional objects, he also set the record for most consecutive bounces on a cribbage board **(1,469)** and an electric guitar **(296)**. He used a conventional table tennis ball to set all records.

Source: http://www.urdb.com

Fastest Rock Band Alphabet

Mick Cullen is a serious audiophile and a volunteer DJ, and boasts a music library of about 26,000 songs. That kind of in-depth knowledge came in handy when Mick set out to establish a hard-to-beat record for reciting the fastest rock band alphabet. To establish the mark, a person must name a rock band for each and every letter of the alphabet, in order. Being a fast talker as well as having a treasure trove of musical knowledge definitely helps, and these skills enabled Mick to go A to Z in a speedy **10.9 SECONDS.**

.....Head Full of Erasers

Sure, you can use erasers to eliminate pencil mistakes... but doesn't balancing them on your head seem like more fun? To liven up the radio show he hosts, Mick Cullen set out to set a new mark in this category. His co-host Carl was enlisted to carefully place the pencil erasers on his head one by one. The final result was a new record of **19 ERASERS** on Mick's head... where they remained while Mick delivered the daily newscast over the airwaves!

Source: http://www.urdb.com

Stow Those CDs:

The record for fastest time to place 19 CDs back in their cases was also born out of Mick Cullen's lively radio show. While the world is swiftly moving to MP3, chances are most people still have a stack of CDs around the house, often mismatched. Mick accomplished the ultimate organization, placing 19 CDs back in their cases in only **1 MINUTE AND 23.5 SECONDS.** The CDS had to be placed in their matching jewel case for the record to count. Mick's love of music allowed him to quickly identify CDs by color and art alone and thus place them in the correct case that much faster.

Candle-Studded Cupcake

New York's David Ross was determined to set a world record by cramming the most birthday candles onto one standard-sized cupcake, but fell just short in an attempt on his 33rd birthday. When July 4, 2010, rolled around, David decided to set the record on America's birthday. The home-baked cupcake was frosted and studded with **235 CANDLES,** which were then lit at the same time. The amount of flame produced a huge fireball that set off the smoke alarm, but all candles were succesfully blown out by the crowd that had gathered to watch the record-setting attempt!

One-Legged Hula Hooping

New York's Ella Morton's pursuit of her world record shows just the kind of determination that is needed to be a record breaker. She first set out to claim the one-legged hula hooping record on stage before a live crowd, but nerves got to her and she fell short. Months later, she tried again and did set a record of just over 3 minutes, but that was quickly broken by over 2 minutes. Determined to reclaim her title, Ella set up a webcam and set the current mark, a full **12 MINUTES AND 1 SECOND** of hopping hula hoop madness! She reported burning calves for days afterward, but it was a small price to pay to become the world's best.

Most People To Pop Bubble Wrap At Once

Few things are more irresistible than a fresh sheet of bubble wrap. Everyone loves the satisfying pop the little air bubbles make when they are squeezed. So finding participants to set the record for most people to pop bubble wrap at once was definitely not a problem. **1,456 PEOPLE** attending the State Fair Meadowlands in New Jersey attacked thirteen rolls of 500-foot-long bubble wrap, popping an incredible total of 2.4 million bubbles!

Balancing Bikes & Stacks of Chairs

Springfield, IL's Brian Pankey is a master of balancing objects, no matter how challenging. He believes that to appeal to an audience an entertainer should use everyday objects, so he came up with the idea of balancing a bicycle on his forehead. First he had to stop the back wheel from slipping, so he locked the back tire of a 12-speed and gave it a try. The result was a new record of **2 MINUTES AND 48 SECONDS.** Not content with this record, he then stacked six folding chairs one on top of the other, got on his knees, and balanced the entire stack on his chin for **56.95 SECONDS.**

Source: http://www.urdb.com, http://www.njcreativedirection.com

Taking It on the Chin

After having succesfully set records balancing light objects, Brian Pankey decided to move on to the heavy stuff, namely sofas and box springs! As an experienced performer, he made sure the record was set safely, but that doesn't mean it was easy. A unique mixture of balance and raw strength is needed for this type of record, as the would-be record-breaker can have no help lifting the objects to be balanced. First up was a 60-pound queen sized box spring, which he managed to balance on his chin for **14 SECONDS.** Next, he really gave his neck muscles a workout by chin-balancing a sofa weighing 75 pounds for **7 EXCRUCIATING SECONDS!**

Beanbag Juggling

Juggling takes skill, practice, and dedication. Just ask multiple record holder Brian Pankey. Inspired by his 9th-grade history teacher, Brian took up juggling and did odd jobs to earn money to buy supplies from the local magic store. The hard work paid off with a junior national juggling championship at age 16, and he's still at it today. He performs accross the Midwest and is always looking for new things to incorporate in his act... like beanbags! When shoppers at a retail store where he tried them out broke out in applause, he knew he had a winner. Brian managed to juggle three 30-inch, 3-pound beanbags for **57 SECONDS.**

Flaming Juggle on Moving Platform

If you've ever tried juggling, you know it can be difficult. Now picture trying it on a moving platform! Brian Pankey does just that with flaming tennis balls, all while balancing on a rola bola. Consisting of a plank resting on top of a cylinder, a rola bola requires great balance and concentration when a person remains relatively still. Add in the arm swinging that juggling requires, and most people would last only a few seconds before losing their balance. Despite the obstacles, Brian (wearing canvas work gloves) juggled three tennis balls lit on fire and made **79 CONSECUTIVE CATCHES** before the heat got to him... all while balancing on the moving rola bola.

Source: http://www.urdb.com

Most Fireballs in 30 seconds

In addition to juggling and balancing, Brian Pankey has another amazing trick up his sleeve… fire-breathing. This is a very dangerous activity that takes years of practice, as it's very easy to light your face and hair on fire or swallow a mouthful of lamp oil. But Brian's mastered the art and has set the record for blowing the most fireballs in 30 seconds with **8 FIREBALLS.** To qualify, the fireballs had to reach a height of 13 feet. Brian held a torch in one hand and a thermos of lamp oil in the other, replenishing his mouth between fireballs to breathe fire as rapidly as possible.

Fastest Spelling with Candy

St. Mary's County, MD's Taylor Priest, 16, woke up one morning determined to own a world record. She chose to take on the record for spelling the word "BALL" in all capital letters, using 30 round chocolate candies. Sitting down at her dining room table with a bag of candy, Taylor experimented with many different methods of spelling the word. Once she had the technique, she just needed to refine her speed. Two hours later, Taylor was ready, and set a new world record with a time of **15.28 SECONDS.** After setting the record, Taylor made sure to eat her materials!

Longest Shofar Note

Mitchell Booth of Summit, NJ, realized he had a unique talent that just might make him a record-breaker—he could hold a note on the shofar for an incredibly long time. The shofar, a ram's horn, is difficult to blow, requiring a strong breath and significant stamina. After a few warm-up attempts, Mitchell blew and sustained a clear note for a full **44.8 SECONDS!** Mitchell is still not satisfied, however, and vows to break his record soon.

Source: http://www.urdb.com

Loudest Soda and Antacid Chorus

April 15, 2009, saw a very LOUD record being set. **75 MEMBERS** of Florida's Reflections of Christ Student Ministry became the largest group ever assembled to mix soda and antacid tablets in their mouths. One tablet was put in each kid's mouth, followed by a healthy swig of soda. The two ingredients combine explosively, so much so that the vast majority of the group could only hold the mixture in their mouths for about two minutes, while the hardiest of the competitors lasted almost ten minutes before spitting it out.

Longest Time Hopping on One Leg:

Tyler Rolfe of Lake City, FL, wanted a record that required endurance. When the chance came to compete against others, on stage, for the longest time hopping on one leg, he knew he'd found his challenge. As the other competitors dropped out one by one, Tyler kept right on hopping. Finally he could hop no more, but by then his time of **6 MINUTES AND 13 SECONDS** had shattered the previous record by more than five minutes. An exhausted Tyler said, "If this record is ever broken, there is no way I could break it. I don't know how I did it."

Girl Who Sleeps with Most Stuffed Animals

Lucy Darlene Ryall, age 5, of Kensington, CA, has been building her stuffed animal collection for five straight years, but it was only in 2011 that both she and her bed could handle sleeping with all **53 ANIMALS.** She first attempted to set a record in 2006 but it ended badly, when the 18 animals crowded alongside her flattened her against the bars of her crib. But she kept her ultimate goal of 50 in mind and finally achieved it in 2011. Which has now kick-started her push for 100 animals by early 2013...

GET IN THE ACTION!

Why just read the **BOOK OF EXTREME FACTS** when you can be featured in it yourself? Perhaps this chapter has inspired you to set or share some records of your own, such as:

• Tricky balancing acts, like a watermelon on your head!
• Fun with food, like tallest sandwich or marshmallow towers!
• Two-in-one records, like playing a ukulele on a unicycle!

Remember, you are not limited to the above suggestions, or to trying to beat other records in this chapter. Entirely new records are not only allowed… they are encouraged! The only limit is your own creativity. So have some fun (but always remember to keep it SAFE), and if you are younger than 18 remember to ask your parents for permission before attempting any record.

To submit a record:

-Go to *www.bookofextremefacts.com*

-Click on the "Submit New Record" tab

-Provide a brief description of your record and your contact info

-If we decide that your record makes the grade, we will contact you for further details and photos or video of your record

It's just that simple! Good luck…
and **KEEP IT EXTREME!**

Involvement in dangerous sports and related activities carries a significant risk of damage to property, personal injury, or death. Please do not endanger yourself or others or take any unnecessary risks. If you choose to participate in dangerous sports or activities in attempting to achieve a distinction that would be recognized in the next edition of the Book of Extreme Facts, which IDW does not recommend, you do so at your own risk. IDW suggests the use of professional instruction before entering into any sports or physical activity. You should become knowledgeable about the risks involved. By submitting information to IDW related to inclusion in a future edition of the Book of Extreme Facts you assume personal responsibility for your actions and agree to indemnify and hold harmless IDW for the consequences of your actions.

IMAGE CREDITS

Page 30 - FASTEST HUMAN CONVEYER BELT
    Photo by Eisenhower Junior High School
Page 31 - TALLEST ICE CREAM CONE
    Photo by Eisenhower Junior High School
Page 31 - LARGEST LOAF OF BREAD
    Photo by Eisenhower Junior High School
Page 32 - MEGA CHAIN Photo by Eisenhower Junior High School
Page 32 - LONGEST BALLOON CHAIN
    Photo by Eisenhower Junior High School
Page 33 - MEGA STRAW Photo by Eisenhower Junior High School
Page 33 - WORLD'S TALLEST PENCIL TOWER
    Photo by Trenton High School
Page 37 - CANDLE-STUDDED CUPCAKE Photo by David Ross
Page 38 - ONE-LEGGED HULA HOOPING Photo by Ella Morton
Page 41 - LOUDEST SODA AND ANTACID CHORUS
    Photo by Ella Morton
Page 41 - GIRL WHO SLEEPS WITH MOST STUFFED ANIMALS
    Photo by Chris Ryall

CHAPTER 3
WEATHER

Hurricane or Typhoon?

The only difference between a hurricane and a typhoon is where it happens. In general, both kinds of storms are called tropical cyclones. If one happens in the Atlantic, it's a hurricane. If it happens in the Pacific, it's a typhoon. Typhoons tend to be stronger, and the strongest ever was 1979's **TYPHOON TIP**. At its peak, Tip's winds reached 190 mph. It was also the largest storm ever recorded, with a diameter of 1,380 miles!

Typhoon Tip
TIROS-N Visible Channel
4KM GHRR PASS
October 14, 1979 0431 UTC

The Deadliest Hurricane

The worst hurricane on record—**HURRICANE SAN CALIXTO II**—hit the Caribbean islands of Barbados, St. Lucia, St. Eustatius, and Martinique in October 1780. More than 22,000 people reportedly died as winds in excess of 200 mph scoured the islands. The next-deadliest Atlantic storm—Hurricane Mitch—killed over 19,000 people in 1998.

The Galveston Hurricane

In 1900, a hurricane all but destroyed the city of Galveston, Texas, killing at least 8,000 people and maybe as many as 12,000. This made it the **DEADLIEST NATURAL DISASTER EVER** in the United States, a record that stands to this day. By contrast, 2005's Hurricane Katrina killed 1,836 people.

Source: http://www.hurricanecenter.com, http://www.nhc.noaa.gov

KRA BOOOM

Thundersnow

On rare occasions, it can actually **THUNDER DURING A SNOWSTORM**. In an average year, this happens less than seven times in the entire United States. Unlike a regular thunderstorm, the snow actually muffles the thunder so it can only be heard from a few miles away.

Hurricane Katrina

In 2005, Hurricane Katrina struck the Gulf Coast of the United States and destroyed a tremendous amount of coastline, including most famously that of New Orleans, Louisiana. Its storm surge hit **ALMOST 28 FEET,** setting the U.S. record, and the wave of water overwhelmed 53 of the city's levees and flooded around 80% of the city. It also broke the damage record with over **$80 BILLION** worth of destruction.

Hottest Spot

DALLOL, ETHIOPIA, holds the record for the highest average temperature on Earth at 106° F. The hottest recorded temperature on the face of the Earth was 135.9° F in **AL 'AZIZIYAH, LIBYA**. It happened on September 13, 1922. The warmest day that North America ever saw was July 10, 1913, when it reached 134° F in **DEATH VALLEY, CALIFORNIA**.

Source: http://www.theweatherprediction.com, http://www.nhc.noaa.gov, http://www.ncdc.noaa.gov

Coldest Spot

OYMYAKON, RUSSIA, holds the record for the lowest average temperature on Earth. Its average high temperature is 16.7° F, and its average low is -8.9° F. When the temperature fell to -90° F on February 6, 1933, Oymyakon also established the record for the coldest temperature in a permanently inhabited spot. The coldest spot on the planet is **VOSTOK STATION, ANTARCTICA,** with an average low of -67° F and a record low of -129° F, but people don't live there year-round.

Whiteout!

In a whiteout, enough snow falls that **VISIBILITY FALLS TO NEARLY ZERO.** Near the poles, it's possible to have a whiteout on a clear day with a snow-covered land under an overcast sky. This is called sector whiteout. The illusion can even obscure mountains and make it impossible to spot the ground from an airplane.

UNBREAKABLE

Earth Has It Easy

Winds on **SATURN** and **NEPTUNE** can gust at more than 900 miles per hour. The surface of **VENUS** is over 860° F. A Martian tornado—known as a dust devil—can stretch up to five miles high. Winter on **PLUTO** can reach −380° F. On **TITAN**, a moon of Saturn, it rains methane.

Solar Weather

Our Sun has weather all its own. **CORONAL MASS EJECTIONS** and **SOLAR FLARES** can disrupt radio signals on Earth and cause the brilliant light shows in the northern and southern skies that we call the aurora borealis and aurora australis. They've even been known to destroy communications satellites.

Source: http://www.ncdc.noaa.gov, http://www.dictionary.com, http://www.spaceweather.com

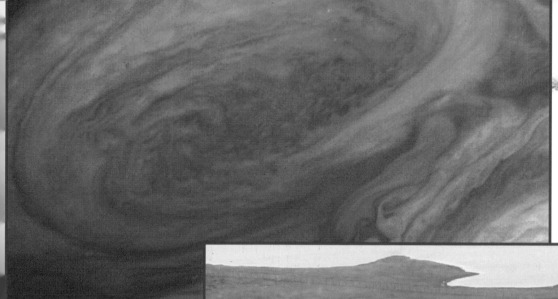

The Great Red Spot

Jupiter has a storm so powerful that we can see it from Earth. Because of its usual color, we know it as the Great Red Spot. It's large enough to swallow three Earths, and it has been raging for **AT LEAST 300 YEARS**. The early astronomer Giovanni Cassini first spotted it in 1665 with a handmade telescope.

American Extremes

The coldest and driest city in the U.S. is **BARROW, ALASKA,** the northernmost city in the nation. Its average temperature is a chilly 10° F, and it only sees 5 inches of precipitation every year. On the other end of the spectrum sits **HAWAII,** which gets over 100 inches of rain every year and has an average yearly temperature over 65° F.

Sun or Rain?

The sunniest city in the U.S. is **YUMA, ARIZONA.** It gets about 90% of its maximum potential sunshine, and it only sees about 3 inches of rain each year. **JUNEAU, ALASKA,** is the cloudiest city in the U.S. It only gets about 30% of the sunshine that it could. Nearby **YAKUTAT, ALASKA,** gets the most rain: over 160 inches.

NEWS YOU CAN USE

The UV Index

The UV (ultraviolet) index can tell you how likely you are to get a sunburn if you go outside. It starts at 0 and usually tops out around 11. However, places in Australia have recorded UV indices **AS HIGH AS 17.** That's a real scorcher!

Source: http://www.space.com, http://www.USAToday.com

Staying Dry

The driest spot in the world is **ARICA, CHILE**. Known as "the City of Eternal Spring," it only gets about 0.03 inches of rain every year, despite the fact that it is a port city that sits on the edge of the Pacific Ocean. Average high temperatures remain between 65° F and 80° F all year round, and the ocean keeps the humidity comfortable, despite the lack of rain.

Getting Wet

The wettest spot in the world— at least on supposedly dry land— is likely **LLORÓ, COLOMBIA,** which gets over 523 inches of rain every year. That's over 43 and a half feet! *Lloró* means "it cried/rained" in Spanish, although the town was supposedly named after a pre-Columbian chief called Gioró.

Monster Sinkholes

In May 2010, during Tropical Storm Agatha, a gigantic hole appeared in Guatemala City and swallowed a three-story building, killing one man. It spanned **60 FEET ACROSS AND OVER 300 FEET DEEP**. A similar hole appeared nearby in 2007, destroying 12 houses and killing three people. Technically, neither was a sinkhole, as they formed when tropical storms overwhelmed the local storm sewer system.

Source: http://www.ncdc.noaa.gov, http://www.nationalgeographic.com

Raining Fish...

On three different occasions, fish rained from the sky in **LAJAMANU,** a small town in northern Australia, hundreds of miles from the nearest large body of water. It happened in 1974, 2004, and 2010. The spangled perch were still alive when they landed, probably after being swept up into the air by a tornado over the ocean, although no tornadoes were reported.

Red Rain

A **BLOOD-RED RAIN** fell on the Indian state of Kerala in the summer of 2001. It also came in hues of yellow, black, and green. Studies showed that the colors were the result of lichen spores caught in the water. How so many spores got up into the air, though, remains a mystery.

Multiple Rainbows

Rainbows are caused by the refraction of light through water, usually rain falling from the sky. It's possible to find **DOUBLE, TRIPLE, OR EVEN QUADRUPLE RAINBOWS** in nature. In a lab in 1988, scientists managed to produce a 200th-order rainbow by using a pendant water drop and a 50mW laser beam.

Source: http://www.popsci.com, http://www.ntnews.com.au, http://www.atoptics.co.uk

One Hot Year

The year 2010 may have been the hottest known since we started tracking such things, just edging out the temps for 2008. **HEAT RECORDS FELL IN 17 COUNTRIES** in 2010, including sweltering heat waves in Russia, Saudi Arabia, Chad, Kuwait, Sudan, Burma, and Pakistan that killed thousands of people and destroyed countless crops and trees.

Tornado!

The U.S. gets the most tornadoes of any country, about **800 PER YEAR,** and they have been recorded in every state—even Alaska and Hawaii. The winds they bring can reach **250 MILES PER HOUR.** They can happen at any altitude. In 2004, a tornado was recorded at an elevation of 12,000 feet in Sequoia National Park.

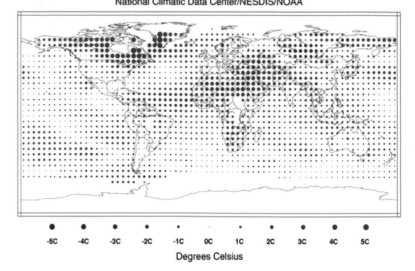

Temperature Anomalies Jan-Dec 2010
(with respect to a 1971-2000 base period)
National Climatic Data Center/NESDIS/NOAA

-5C -4C -3C -2C -1C 0C 1C 2C 3C 4C 5C

Degrees Celsius

NEWS YOU CAN USE

The Eye of the Storm

The center or eye of a cyclonic storm often has **CALM WINDS AND CLEAR SKIES**—surrounded by an eyewall of raging thunderstorms. People sometimes go outside after a storm to discover that they're in the eye. On land, this is safe until the eye moves past and you're engulfed in the storm again. At sea, the eyewall can generate waves over 130 feet high.

Chinese Weather Masters

Before important state visits, Chinese officials often seed the clouds over Beijing with silver iodide, which has a structure similar to ice crystals. This makes the water in the clouds freeze and fall, which creates rain and gives the city excellent weather the next day. China has **A TEAM OF 37,000 PEOPLE** who work at this, most firing mortar shells full of the chemical into the sky.

Source: http://www.guardian.co.uk, http://www.nssl.noaa.gov, http://www.usatoday.com, http://www.sciencedaily.com

Tornado Damage

Tornados can do all sorts of odd damage. They've been known to move buildings off their foundations, strip the asphalt from a road, toss cars over a hundred yards, and even **THROW A 3,000-POUND SAFE A BLOCK AWAY.** They have twisted skyscrapers like the Great Plains Life building in Lubbock, Texas, and destroyed entire towns.

Petrified Lightning

When lightning strikes a sandy beach, it can fuse the sand together instantly to create a tube of natural glass. This is called a **FULGURITE.** It can appear buried up to 50 feet below the surface of the sand, and the longest piece ever recovered was over 16 feet long.

Stuck in the Fog

The **GRAND BANKS** off the coast of Newfoundland, Canada, has been named the foggiest place in the world. This is where the chilly Labrador Current meets the warm Gulf Stream. On average, it sees more than 200 foggy days each year, which doesn't leave much time for sunbathing.

UNBREAKABLE

The Deepest Snow

The snowiest winter in the U.S. happened at the Mt. Baker Ski Area in Washington during the winter of 1998-99. They received **1,140 INCHES OF SNOW** that year—95 feet! This is officially the world record too, but few places outside of the U.S. keep such good records on snowfall, so there could easily be record breakers that went unrecorded.

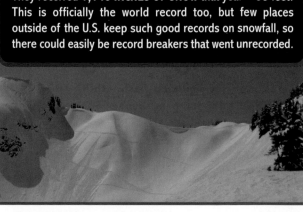

Source: http://www.srh.noaa.gov, http://sciencedaily.com, http://www.amnh.org, http://www.powdermag.com

Fast as Lightning

Lightning travels at **60,000 MILES PER SECOND,** and it heats the air to somewhere between 18,000° F and 60,000° F. The longest bolt measured to date was 118 miles long. When you see lightning, you're actually seeing several strokes happening nearly at once along the same path. A single stroke would be almost too fast to see.

Rolling Thunder

Lightning always produces thunder, even if you might be too far away to actually hear it. Thunder has a rolling sound because it doesn't come from a single point but all along the length of the lightning strike instead. **THE SHARPER THE SOUND, THE CLOSER THE LIGHTNING IS,** and the more it rumbles, the farther away it struck.

Chance of Being Hit By Lightning...

Your chance of being hit by lightning—assuming you are exposed in a situation in which such a strike would even be possible—is around **1 IN 28,500.** About 90% of people struck by lightning survive it, but a quarter of those people suffer from long-term effects.

NEWS YOU CAN USE

The Distance of Lightning

When you see lightning flash, **COUNT THE SECONDS** until you hear thunder. For every five seconds that pass, the lightning is about a mile away. If you continue to track the lightning, you should be able to tell if the storm is getting closer or moving away.

Source: http://www.lightningsafety.com, http://wxdude.com, http://www.lightningsafety.noaa.gov, http://tornadochaser.com

Heavy Hail

The largest hailstone that ever hit the ground in the U.S. fell in Aurora, Nebraska, in 2003. Even after some of it had broken and melted off, it was seven inches across and 18.75 inches around. The heaviest hailstone in the U.S. landed in Coffeyville, Kansas, in 1970. It weighed **1.67 POUNDS.**

Lightning Strikes Several Times

Lightning often strikes in the same place twice, especially if it's drawn to the spot on purpose. The Empire State Building in New York City serves as a lightning rod for the entire area. It gets used in that fashion about **A HUNDRED TIMES** every year.

A World of Lightning

At any given moment, lightning is probably striking someplace on the planet. Earth sees more than **1.4 BILLION** lightning bolts each year, which averages out to roughly **44 TIMES PER SECOND.** The country that takes the most lightning hits every year is the Democratic Republic of Congo.

Source: http://www.nationalgeographic.com, http://www.pbs.org, http://www.weatherquesting.com

Deadly Waters

Seven out of the top ten worst floods in history happened in China. The worst of these came in 1931 when the Yellow River, Yangtze River, and Huai River broke their banks, and the waters killed somewhere **BETWEEN 2.5 MILLION AND 3.7 MILLION PEOPLE.** The flood around the Yellow River alone covered over 20 million acres.

The Power of the Wind

We have used windmills to harness the power of the wind since at least the 1st century. Today, we use farms filled with massive wind turbines to generate a great deal of pollution-free electricity. The largest wind turbine in the world towers over Zaragoza, Spain, and the diameter of its rotors is **NEARLY 420 FEET.**

Heavy Rain

The heaviest rainfall in the world came from Tropical Cyclone Hyacinthe. In one 24-hour period in January 1980, it dropped six feet of rain on La Reunion Island, off the coast of Madagascar in the Indian Ocean. Over the course of five days, it hit the tiny island with **JUST OVER 14 FEET.** That'd fill a lot of swimming pools.

Source: http://epicdisasters.com, http://inhabitat.com, http://www.aoml.noaa.gov

...Frozen at the Equator

Generally, the closer you get to the equator the warmer it gets. However, altitude can affect temperatures as much as latitudes. Mt. Cotopaxi in Ecuador is the highest active volcano in the world. With its peak at 19,348 feet, it is cold enough to sport the only **EQUATORIAL GLACIER** in the world.

UNBREAKABLE

Worst Weather in the World

MOUNT WASHINGTON in New Hampshire is widely regarded as having the worst weather in the world. The fastest wind gust on land was recorded here in 1934 at 231 miles per hour, and it held that record for decades. High winds, freezing temperatures, thick blizzards, impenetrable fog, and barely any calm days make for a rotten year there.

The Hardest Winds

The fastest wind speed ever recorded on Earth was **318 MILES PER HOUR.** This happened while a tornado zipped through the Oklahoma City, Oklahoma, area back in 1999. On average, the windiest place is Commonwealth Bay, along the Antarctic coast. Winds there regularly gust over 200 miles per hour.

NEWS YOU CAN USE

Staying Safe

Modern meteorology allows us to predict the weather days or even weeks in advance. The best way to avoid dangerous weather is to know about it before it happens. The National Oceanic and Atmospheric Administration (NOAA) has **OVER 1,000 RADIO STATIONS** across the U.S. that broadcast severe weather alerts to any NOAA Weather Radio.

Source: http://peaklist.org, http://antarcticconnection.com, MountWashington.org, http://www.nws.noaa.gov

GET IN THE ACTION!

Why just read the **BOOK OF EXTREME FACTS** when you can be featured in it yourself? Perhaps this chapter has inspired you to set or share some records of your own, such as:

• Temperature extremes, like ice-cold summer days or sultry winter days!
• Strange weather phenomena, such as ice-coated streets you can skate on!
• Examples of the destructive force of Mother Nature at her most furious!

Remember, you are not limited to the above suggestions, or to trying to beat other records in this chapter. Entirely new records are not only allowed... they are encouraged! The only limit is your own creativity. So have some fun (but always remember to keep it SAFE), and if you are younger than 18 remember to ask your parents for permission before attempting any record.

To submit a record:

-Go to *www.bookofextremefacts.com*

-Click on the "Submit New Record" tab

-Provide a brief description of your record and your contact info

-If we decide that your record makes the grade, we will contact you for further details and photos or video of your record

It's just that simple! Good luck...
and **KEEP IT EXTREME!**

Involvement in dangerous sports and related activities carries a significant risk of damage to property, personal injury or death. Please do not endanger yourself or others or take any unnecessary risks. If you choose to participate in dangerous sports or activities in attempting to achieve a distinction that would be recognized in the next edition of Extreme Facts, which IDW does not recommend, you do so at your own risk. IDW suggests the use of professional instruction before entering into any sports or physical activity. You should become knowledgeable about the risks involved. By submitting information to IDW related to inclusion in a future edition of Extreme Facts you assume personal responsibility for your actions and agree to indemnify and hold harmless IDW for the consequences of your actions.

IMAGE CREDITS

Page 45 - HOTTEST SPOT Photo by Rolf Cosar
Page 47 - AMERICAN EXTREMES Photo by Dave Cohoe
Page 48 - STAYING DRY Photo by Heretiq
Page 49 - MULTIPLE RAINBOWS Photo by Adrian Michael
Page 51 - STUCK IN THE FOG Photo by Aconcagua
Page 51 - PETRIFIED LIGHTNING Photo by Ji-Elle
Page 51 - THE DEEPEST SNOW Photo by Wavepacke
Page 53 - LIGHTNING STRIKES SEVERAL TIMES Photo by Raul Heinrich
Page 55 - WORST WEATHER IN THE WORLD Photo by BenFrantzDale

CHAPTER 4
THE WORLD

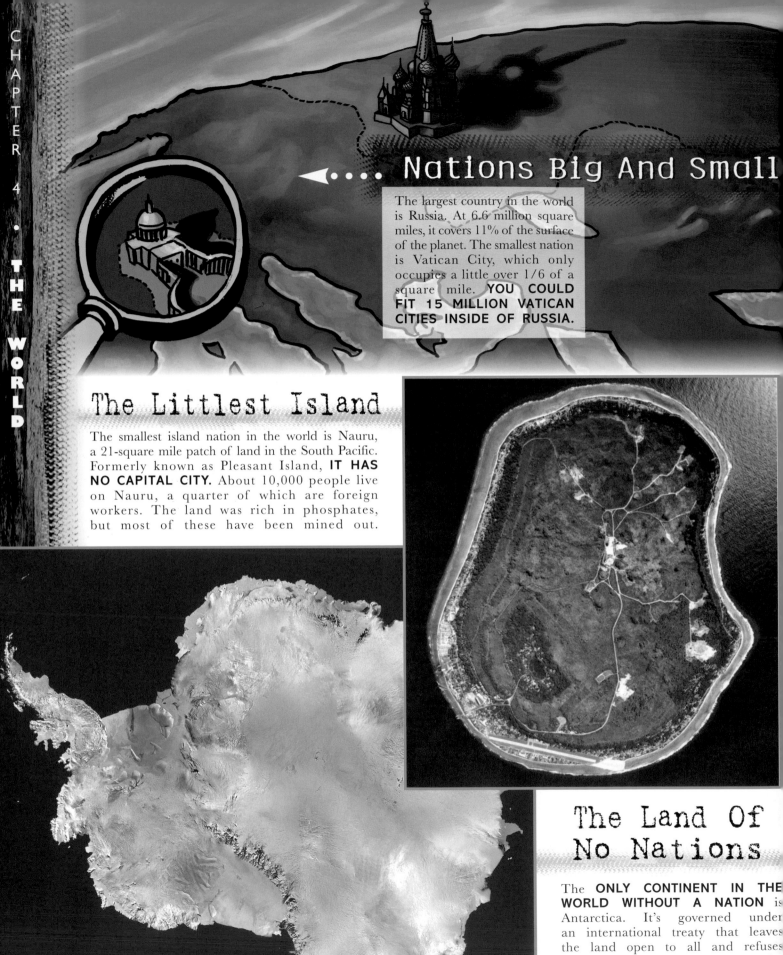

◄···· Nations Big And Small

The largest country in the world is Russia. At 6.6 million square miles, it covers 11% of the surface of the planet. The smallest nation is Vatican City, which only occupies a little over 1/6 of a square mile. **YOU COULD FIT 15 MILLION VATICAN CITIES INSIDE OF RUSSIA.**

The Littlest Island

The smallest island nation in the world is Nauru, a 21-square mile patch of land in the South Pacific. Formerly known as Pleasant Island, **IT HAS NO CAPITAL CITY.** About 10,000 people live on Nauru, a quarter of which are foreign workers. The land was rich in phosphates, but most of these have been mined out.

The Land Of No Nations

The **ONLY CONTINENT IN THE WORLD WITHOUT A NATION** is Antarctica. It's governed under an international treaty that leaves the land open to all and refuses to recognize any claims to the land made by any existing country. The next least-governed place is Australia, which only has one nation on the entire continent

Source: Source: http://www.nationsonline.org, https://www.cia.gov

Beware! Exploding Cucumber!

More properly a gourd, the squirting cucumber spreads its seeds like no other plant—**BY EXPLODING!** When the prickly bluish-green fruit of this plant reaches maturity, it detaches from the stem of the plant. That's when things really get weird. It forcibly ejects its seeds in a powerful spray of mucus-like juice that typically travels 10 to 20 feet! This is one cucumber you're better off staying far away from.

A Big Stinker

Found originally in the rainforests of Sumatra, the titan arum—a plant also known as **THE CORPSE FLOWER**—bears the largest bloom in the world. It can reach six feet high and open up to four feet wide. Unfortunately, it's also the stinkiest flower around. It attracts flies to pollinate it by smelling like a ripe carcass.

A Sea Of Weeds....

In the middle of the Bermuda Triangle sits a monstrous tangle of sargassum, a type of seaweed that floats free on the ocean's surface. First **DISCOVERED BY CHRISTOPHER COLUMBUS,** this relatively calm region of the ocean ensnared many sailing ships during the Age of Sail, and ships fell to disaster in it as recently as 1982.

Source: http://www.britannica.com, http://www.huntington.org,
http://www.bermuda-triangle.org

America's Longest War

The Afghan War, begun in October 2001, is America's longest-running war. In June 2010, it broke the record set by the U.S.' involvement in the Vietnam War, which lasted for 103 months, **OVER EIGHT AND A HALF YEARS.** By contrast, the U.S. involvement in World War II lasted less than four full years.

Mixed-Up Days

The International Date Line is an imaginary line that runs through the Pacific Ocean. The time on the east of the line is always a day later than the time on the west. **THE LINE ISN'T STRAIGHT,** though. Even though Samoa lies to the southwest of Kiribati, it's 25 hours later in Samoa than it is in Kiribati.

..A Crowded Earth

With more than **1.3 BILLION CITIZENS,** China has more people than any other country on Earth. Only India even comes close, with nearly 1.2 billion people within its borders. That's about four times as many people as live in the United States (#3). The nation with the fewest people is Vatican City, with 829 citizens, although the Pitcairn Islands (an Australian territory) has only 48.

NEWS YOU CAN USE

Living Longer

People in Monaco have the longest life expectancy. A child born there can **EXPECT TO LIVE NEARLY 90 YEARS.** A child born in Angola, on the other hand, might not expect to make it to even 39 years old. Kids born in the U.S. should live to just over 78 years old.

Source: http://abcnews.go.com, http://www.worldatlas.com, https://www.cia.gov

Finding Work

With unemployment hovering around 9%, times might seem tough in the U.S., and compared to Monaco—which has zero unemployment—they probably are. Count your blessings that things aren't as bad in America as they are in Zimbabwe, where the best guess is that **THE UNEMPLOYMENT RATE IS AROUND 95%!**

Reading Well

Several countries claim that all of their citizens are able to read. That's a literacy level of 100%. In the U.S., **WE'RE NOT QUITE PERFECT,** only reaching 99%. The worst nation in the world for literacy is Burkina Faso, in which less than 22% of its people can read. The next worst is Afghanistan, which has a literacy rate of just over 28%.

That's Fast!

The Earth is faster than anything that might be on it. Things on its equator—including people—**MOVE AROUND 1,000 MILES PER HOUR** just due to the planet's rotation. You can add to that just by walking to the east, but you only perceive how you move relative to the rest of the planet. To top it off, the Earth also speeds around the sun at a dizzying 66,700 miles per hour.

UNBREAKABLE
On Earth

The biggest thing on Earth is the Earth itself. All told, the planet weighs about 6,547,000,000,000,000,000,000—or 6.5 sextillion—tons. It's around 4.6 billion years old, nearly 25,000 miles around at the equator, and has about 57,392,928 square miles of land.

Source: https://www.cia.gov, http://www.nationmaster.com, http://imagine.gsfc.nasa.gov, http://www.worldatlas.com

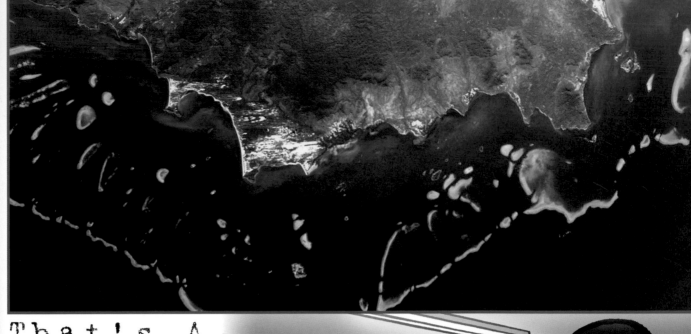

That's A Lot Of Coral

The Great Barrier Reef off the shores of Australia is the largest coral reef in the world. It's actually nearly 3,000 reefs clustered together over a 33,000-square-mile stretch of land that is 1,600 miles across at its widest point. Estimates of the age of various parts of the reef range from 20,000 to **HALF A MILLION YEARS OLD.**

NEWS YOU CAN USE

Pierce that Ear, Sailor!

Since ancient times, sailors have pierced their ears to show that they've either traveled around the world or crossed the equator. They also wore valuable earrings so that if they drowned and someone found their body the jewelry could help pay for a decent burial—**OR AT LEAST KEEP IT AWAY FROM THE SHARKS.**

Go Long! Go Large!

Democracy as we know it was founded in the United States. By some measures, the U.S. has the longest-lasting government still around today, having been established by the Constitution in 1789. The **LARGEST DEMOCRACY IN THE WORLD,** however, is the Republic of India, which has been operating since India declared its independence from Great Britain in 1947.

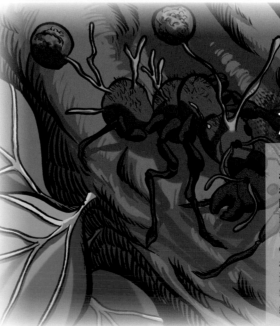

Zombie Ants

Harvard scientists have discovered a fungus that infects carpenter ants and **TAKES OVER THEIR BRAINS!** As it kills an ant, the fungus forces it to find the underside of a leaf and bite hard enough to fasten itself in a place and position from which it can infect other ants. Wilder still, fossil evidence shows this has been going on for 48 million years.

Source: http://www.beyondbooks.com, http://www.guardian.co.uk, http://www.extremescience.com, Encyclopedia of Body Adornment

Would You Like Some Salt With That?

The Dead Sea in Jordan is the saltiest body of water in nature. By some measurements, it's ten times saltier than the oceans, and salt crystallizes on the rocks along its shores. That's probably because these shores are the lowest point of dry land on the planet, sitting **OVER 1,300 FEET BELOW SEA LEVEL.**

The Fortress Of Crystals

In 2000, miners in Mexico discovered a cave filled with some of the largest natural crystals ever discovered. **THE CAVE OF CRYSTALS**—which looks something like The Fortress of Solitude from the Superman films—sits a thousand feet underground and features bolts of transparent gypsum that weigh up to 55 tons and stretch up to 36 feet long.

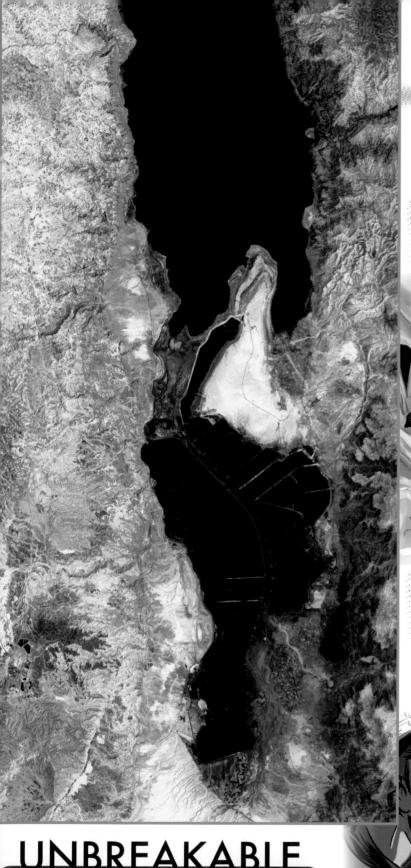

Make It Quick!

The shortest recorded war in the history of the world was the Anglo-Zanzibar War. It was fought the morning of August 27, 1896, and **IT BARELY LASTED 38 MINUTES.** The sultan ruling Zanzibar for the British had died, and when his nephew tried to seize power, five British warships shelled the palace until the nephew and his forces gave up.

UNBREAKABLE

King for Life

It's hard running a country. No one did it for longer, though, than King Sobhuza II of Swaziland in southern Africa. He inherited his title when he was only five months old and **HELD IT UNTIL HIS DEATH ALMOST 83 YEARS LATER.** During his reign, he negotiated for peaceful independence from Great Britain, which officially happened on September 6, 1968.

Source: http://www.wired.com, http://www.visitjordan.com, http://www.sntc.org.sz, http://www.bbc.co.uk

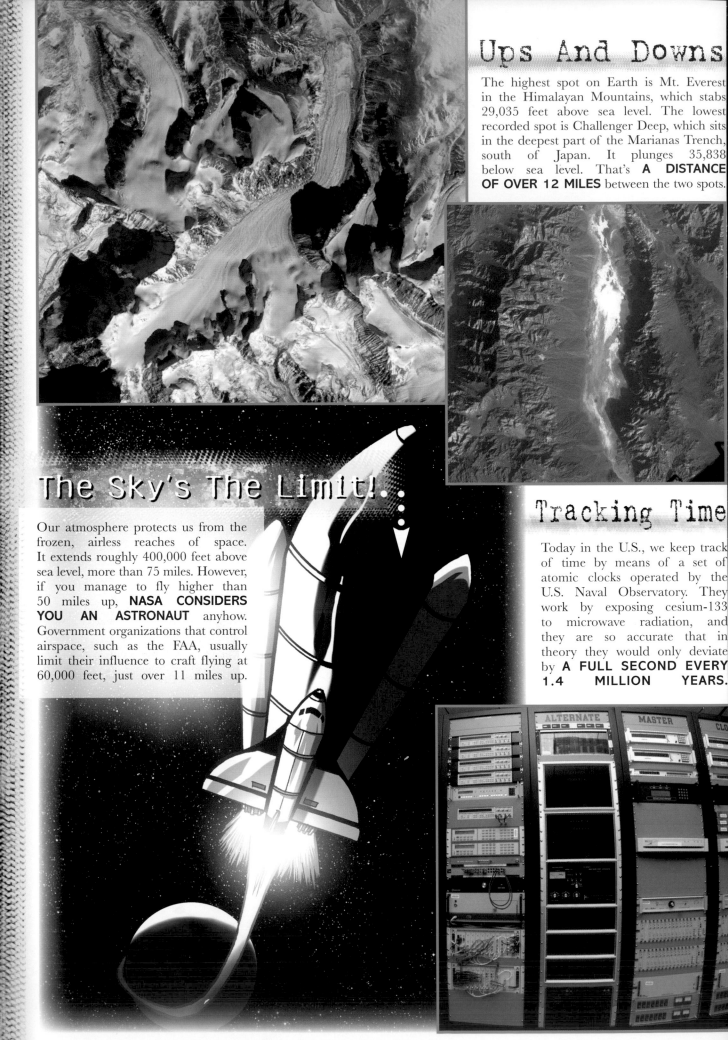

Ups And Downs

The highest spot on Earth is Mt. Everest in the Himalayan Mountains, which stabs 29,035 feet above sea level. The lowest recorded spot is Challenger Deep, which sits in the deepest part of the Marianas Trench, south of Japan. It plunges 35,838 below sea level. That's **A DISTANCE OF OVER 12 MILES** between the two spots.

The Sky's The Limit!...

Our atmosphere protects us from the frozen, airless reaches of space. It extends roughly 400,000 feet above sea level, more than 75 miles. However, if you manage to fly higher than 50 miles up, **NASA CONSIDERS YOU AN ASTRONAUT** anyhow. Government organizations that control airspace, such as the FAA, usually limit their influence to craft flying at 60,000 feet, just over 11 miles up.

Tracking Time

Today in the U.S., we keep track of time by means of a set of atomic clocks operated by the U.S. Naval Observatory. They work by exposing cesium-133 to microwave radiation, and they are so accurate that in theory they would only deviate by **A FULL SECOND EVERY 1.4 MILLION YEARS.**

Source: http://www.extremescience.com

The earth doesn't quite take a full 24 hours to make a complete rotation on its axis. It's actually **23 HOURS, 54 MINUTES, AND 4 SECONDS.** However, the planet isn't just rotating, it's also orbiting the sun. The extra movement from moving along the earth's orbit makes up for the missing 5 minutes and 56 seconds each day.

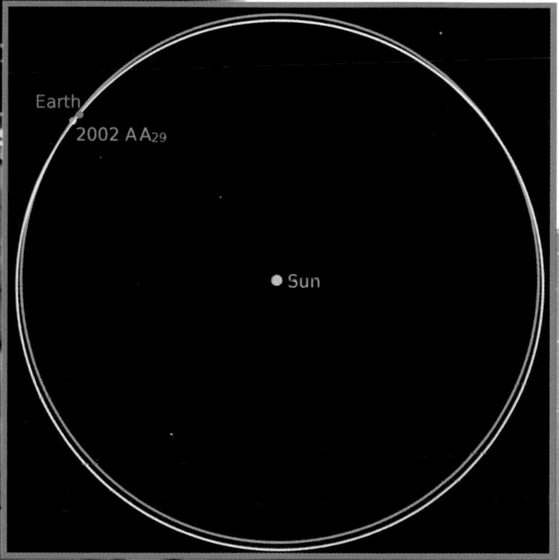

Earth
2002 AA$_{29}$
● Sun

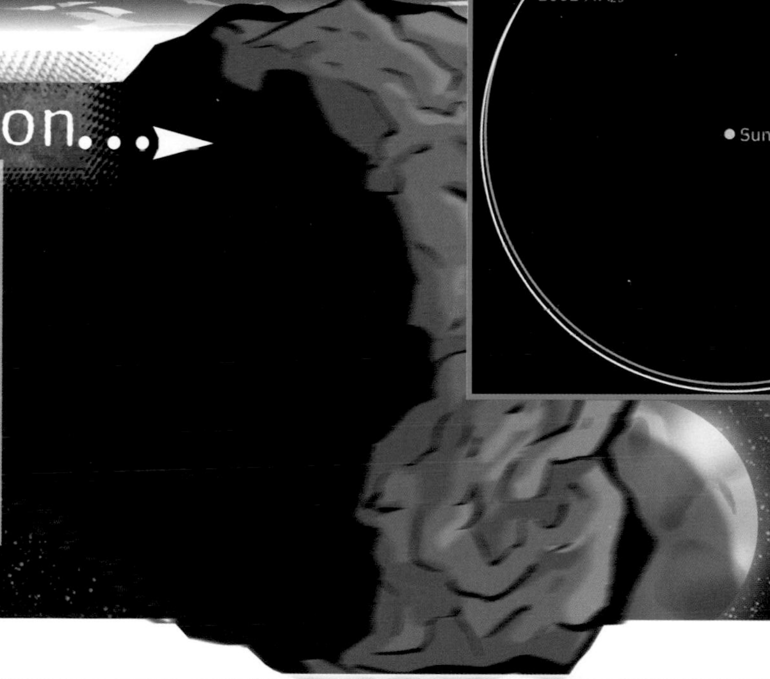

That's No Moon...

Two large, natural rocks **FOLLOW THE EARTH AROUND ITS ORBIT**— and we're not talking about the Moon, which orbits the Earth, not the Sun. The asteroid 3753 Cruithne—which is only 3 miles across—orbits the sun in a path close to that of Earth's. Asteroid 2002 AA29 is much smaller— less than 200 feet across—but it follows our orbit, too.

Longer Days

A billion years ago, the Moon was closer to the Earth and took only 20 days to orbit it, rather than the 29.5 days we see today. **A DAY ON EARTH WAS A MERE 18 HOURS** back then, rather than our traditional 24. The tidal forces of the Moon slow down the Earth's rotation over the course of millions of years, accounting for the current length of our day. At the same time, the Moon moves about 1.6 inches farther away from the Earth every year.

Source: http://www.universetoday.com, http://www.space.com

The Highest Tides

Tides go from high to low every 6 hours and 13 minutes. The Bay of Fundy in eastern Canada has the biggest shift in tides on the planet. On average, the tides rise and fall over 50 feet with each cycle. Adventure guides offer rafting tours that ride the surges of water—called **TIDAL BORES**—up and down the bay.

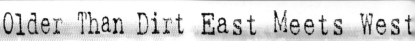

Older Than Dirt

The oldest living thing on Earth is a unique plant called King's lomatia—a special species of King's holly—sprawling in a protected rain forest in Tasmania. Scientists believe it may actually be **43,000 YEARS OLD!** Some of the leaves fallen from it are so old that they've become fossils in the ground near the plant!

East Meets West

The easternmost and westernmost points of the United States are **BOTH LOCATED IN ALASKA'S ALEUTIAN ISLANDS.** The most easterly point (Pochnoi Point on Semisopochnoi Island) is only about 70 miles from the most westerly point (Amatignak Island), but the 180th meridian—the line that separates the Earth's Eastern and Western Hemispheres—falls right between them!

Source: http://www.bayoffundytourism.com, http://www.commerce.state.ak.us, http://www.sciencemag.org

Short-Timers

The shortest-lived animal is the mayfly, the adult form of which has an average lifespan of less than a single day. Depending on the species of mayfly, it can be much shorter than that, down to **JUST 30 MINUTES!** That gives it just enough time to mate before it dies—if it's lucky!

Falling Stardust....

The Earth coalesced out of stardust billions of years ago, but there's still a lot of that stuff out there. These free-floating particles are captured by the Earth's gravity and pulled down to the planet on a constant basis. By some estimates, the Earth gathers **UP TO 30,000 TONS OF COSMIC DUST** every year.

The Frog-Eating Plant

The common bladderwort is an aquatic plant that uses special underwater bladders to suck in its prey and **DIGEST IT ALIVE.** These are large enough to capture mosquito larvae, fish fry, and even tiny tadpoles (baby frogs). Smaller victims can be consumed quickly and allow the plant to reset its trap in as little as 15 minutes.

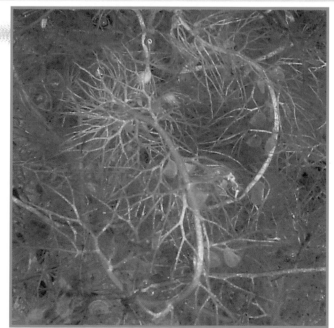

NEWS YOU CAN USE

Your Universal Address

You can probably write your address all the way from your street, city, state, nation, planet, and even solar system (hint: it's the Solar System), but where do you go from there? The Solar System sits in the Orion Arm of the Milky Way galaxy, which is part of the Virgo Supercluster, **ALL PART OF THE UNIVERSE.**

Source: http://www.agriculture.purdue.edu, http://www.jpl.nasa.gov, http://www.dnr.state.wi.us, http://www.nationsonline.org

Large, Deep Holes

The Grand Canyon is the one of the largest canyons on the face of the Earth, but it's not even the deepest one in America. That honor goes to **HELLS CANYON,** near where Washington, Oregon, and Idaho meet. At its deepest point, it's 7,993 feet from bottom to top. The deepest in the world is the Cotahuasi Canyon in Peru, and it's 11,003 feet deep.

A Stone Raft

Pumice is a special kind of volcanic rock filled with enough air pockets that it can actually float on water. After a volcanic eruption, enough pumice can collect in the water to form **A PUMICE RAFT.** Some scientists believe that this is one way to explain how plants and animals may have traveled between the continents.

Beneath A Blood-Red Moon

During a lunar eclipse, the Earth passes directly between the Sun and the full Moon. As the light from the Sun passes around the Earth, the Earth's atmosphere bends the light and turns it red, just like it does for a sunrise or sunset. When the light hits the Moon, it **MAKES IT GLOW RED.** This happens a couple times a year, but it's only visible from part of the planet each time.

Source: http://geology.com, http://science.nasa.gov, http://earthobservatory.nasa.gov

A Big Rock From The Sky

About 80,000 years ago, the world's largest meteorite fell to Earth in what is today the African country of Namibia. It's a sandwich-shaped slab of iron and nickel that forms a 9-foot square that's 3 feet thick and weighs **A WHOPPING 66 TONS.** Amazingly, there's no crater where it fell, possibly because its unusual shape slowed its descent.

UNBREAKABLE

The Smallest Flower

The smallest flowers in the world come from a type of duckweed called wolffia. The whole plant is the size of a long grain of rice, and a full bouquet of its flowers is **smaller than a pencil's eraser.** Despite this, it's an excellent source of protein, and fish farmers use it as a food that also helps to keep the water clean.

The Most Active Volcano

The top contender for most active volcano in the world is Kilauea, which sits in the southeast of Hawaii. From 1952 to 1982, it erupted 53 times. It last erupted in January 1983, but **IT HASN'T STOPPED SINCE!** No wonder Pele, the Hawaiian volcano goddess, calls Kilauea her home.

Long Way From Anywhere

The most remote island in the world is a tiny, uninhabited Norwegian territory called Bouvet Island. It sits between Africa and Antarctica, and it's **1,404 MILES AWAY** from the nearest place with any people. That place—Tristan da Cunha, population 271—is the most remote place with any permanent inhabitants.

Source: http://earthobservatory.nasa.gov, http://hvo.wr.usgs.gov

GET IN THE ACTION!

Why just read the **BOOK OF EXTREME FACTS** when you can be featured in it yourself? Perhaps this chapter has inspired you to set or share some records of your own, such as:

• Unique facts about your town or state that set it apart from all the rest!
• Natural wonders found nowhere else on Earth!
• Weird and wonderful plants native to your area!

Remember, you are not limited to the above suggestions, or to trying to beat other records in this chapter. Entirely new records are not only allowed… they are encouraged! The only limit is your own creativity. So have some fun (but always remember to keep it SAFE), and if you are younger than 18 remember to ask your parents for permission before attempting any record.

To submit a record:

-Go to *www.bookofextremefacts.com*

-Click on the "Submit New Record" tab

-Provide a brief description of your record and your contact info

-If we decide that your record makes the grade, we will contact you for further details and photos or video of your record

It's just that simple! Good luck…
and **KEEP IT EXTREME!**

Involvement in dangerous sports and related activities carries a significant risk of damage to property, personal injury or death. Please do not endanger yourself or others or take any unnecessary risks. If you choose to participate in dangerous sports or activities in attempting to achieve a distinction that would be recognized in the next edition of Extreme Facts, which IDW does not recommend, you do so at your own risk. IDW suggests the use of professional instruction before entering into any sports or physical activity. You should become knowledgeable about the risks involved. By submitting information to IDW related to inclusion in a future edition of Extreme Facts you assume personal responsibility for your actions and agree to indemnify and hold harmless IDW for the consequences of your actions.

IMAGE CREDITS

Page 59 - BEWARE! EXPLODING CUCUMBER Photo by RickP
Page 59 - A BIG STINKER by Patche99z
Page 66 - THE HIGHEST TIDES Photo by gwydionwilliams
Page 66 - OLDER THAN DIRT Photo by Shantavira
Page 67 - SHORT-TIMERS Photo by Luc Viatour
Page 68 - LARGE, DEEP HOLES Photo by Art Bromage
Page 69 - THE SMALLEST FLOWER Photo by Christian Fischer

CHAPTER 5
ANIMALS

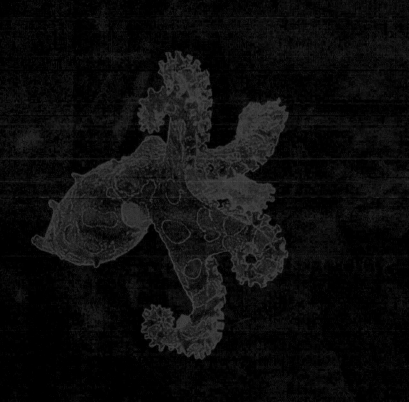

Nature's Biggest Tongues

Evolution has produced many weird and wonderful adaptations, with some truly bizarre results. The award for the longest tongue in proportion to its body goes to *Anoura fistulata*, the **TUBE-LIPPED NECTAR BAT**. In order to get at the nectar hidden deep within flowers, its tongue is one and a half times the size of its body! Other extremely long tongues in nature can be found in **CHAMELEONS** and **GIRAFFES**. For overall tongue size, the champion is the world's largest animal, the **BLUE WHALE**.

Frozen Frog

In the cold Northern forests of Canada, the **WOOD FROG** has a unique way of surviving the harsh winter—it freezes solid. It winters on land, nestling under wet leaf litter on the forest floor. When the litter freezes, so does the frog—its heart stops beating, ice encases its internal organs, and its blood freezes solid. Long, flat ice crystals even form between the skin and muscles. Come the spring thaw, the wood frog is no worse for wear, emerging to fill the forest with its chirping chorus up to a month before its aquatic-based cousins.

Dart-Shooting Slug

When it comes to attracting a mate, the **GREEN AND YELLOW SLUG** of Borneo has a novel approach… it uses a harpoon-shaped dart. This curious creature lives high up in mountainous forests and sports a tail three times as long as its head. It has a tiny shell, one far too small to allow the slug to retract its body inside. When mating season approaches, it fires a hormone-injecting calcium-carbonate dart into a potential partner, hoping to attract its attention. Ouch!

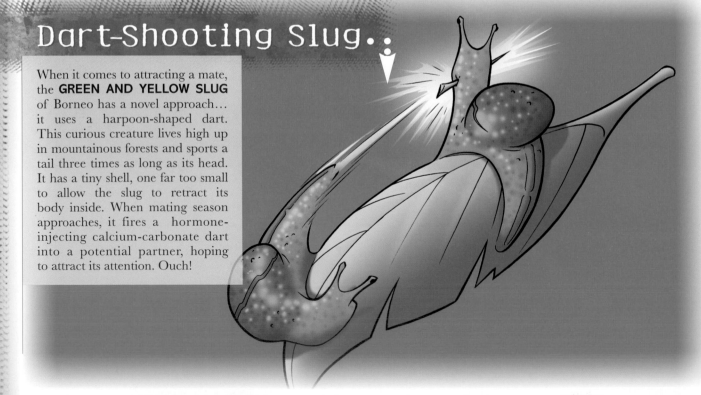

Source: http://news.bbc.co.uk, http://www.naturenorth.com, http://www.livescience.com

... Massive Bugs

Insects exists in the teeming millions in every corner of the globe, with untold numbers of species just waiting to be discovered. And that's a scary thought, considering what we know is out there already. Consider the **GOLIATH BEETLE,** the biggest insect in the world. There are insects that are larger (although at 4 1/2 inches, it's pretty big!), but none with a bigger mass than this 3.2 ounce behemoth. The longest bug is a type of **GIANT STICK INSECT** that lives in the rainforests of Borneo and measures 20 inches long!

Worldwide Webs

The thought of being surrounded by spiders is not exactly a comforting one, but it's a fact. It's estimated that you are never more than 3 to 10 feet away from a spider… and an estimated 1 million spiders live in each acre of land. Most are small and eat huge amounts of insects—more than bats and birds combined. The **GOLIATH BIRD-EATING SPIDER** is a different sort… this giant can grow up to 11 inches long and feasts on birds, bats, lizards, and frogs. It's harmless to humans, and can even warn you of its whereabouts by rattling the hairs on its body to produce a loud hiss.

Fastest Animals On Turf

"Speed kills" is an old saying, and in nature it holds true. But speed also saves in the wild, allowing prey to escape predators. Whether for fight or flight, these are the fastest land animals nature has produced: the **OSTRICH** is the fastest bird, with a top speed of 40+ mph; the **SPINY-TAILED IGUANA,** at 21 mph, is the fastest reptile; the **CHEETAH** holds the mammal record with an amazing 60+ mph speed; and the **COCKROACH** is the speediest insect, rushing for safety at just over 5 mph.

Source: http://www.extremescience.com, http://biology.suite101.com, http://animals.howstuffworks.com

Red Sweat

The **HIPPOPOTAMUS,** a huge relative of the hog that spends most of its life in the water, may be a strict vegetarian, but that doesn't mean its gentle. Far from it... hippos are always battling each other, resulting in many wounds and scratches. But these wounds never get infected, and scientists have discovered the reason why... its due to the animals unique red "sweat." Far from being blood (as the ancients thought), this miraculous substance is made up of red and orange pigment. The red pigment is a strong antibiotic, while both are UV-blocking substances, meaning the hippo provides its own sunscreen!

Man-Sized Salamander...

Salamanders can often be found hiding under rocks, but don't expect to find a **CHINESE GIANT SALAMANDER** there... it's the size of a human being! This strange, flat creature can grow to an incredible 5' 10" and spends its life underwater. As an amphibian, it needs to breathe air, but it lacks gills. This problem is solved by its unique skin. Rough and porous, the skin helps the creature to respirate. Its North American cousin, the **HELLBENDER,** can grow up to 2 feet long and was once common throughout the eastern United States.

Toxic Spit And Starry Nose....

Moles are well known to gardners, burrowing underground with their strong, curved claws in search of food. Once a tasty earthworm is found, the mole uses toxic saliva to immobilize its prey for later eating. The most bizzare of all moles lives in Canada and the eastern U.S.— the **STAR-NOSED MOLE**. This hand-sized creature sports a nose consisting of 22 tentacles, making it look like its face just exploded! The nose tentacles move like searching fingers and help the mole find worms burrowing in wet mud. When the mole eats, the tentacles bunch up like a fist to get out of the way of its mouth.

Source: http://www.arkive.org, http://www.hellbenders.org, http://www.enature.com, http://news.bbc.co.uk

Snakes In The Air

To many people, snakes inspire stark terror. Although most are practically deaf and nearly blind, they possess razor-sharp teeth and, in some cases, deadly venom. But as long as you watch your step, you're OK… its not like they can fly, right? Bad news... some can. Four species of tree snake are adept at gliding long distances, and launch themselves into space in search of prey. One species, the **PARADISE TREE SNAKE**, can even turn in the air! Luckily, the mild venom secreted by these snakes would only be dangerous to you if you were a mouse or other small animal.

Quarter-Sized Snake

Rattlesnakes striking with fangs bared, cobras spitting into the eyes of their prey, and enormous pythons crushing hapless victims don't tell the whole story of snakes. There are, after all, 3,000+ species in the wild! On the far edge of the size spectrum is the **THREAD SNAKE,** *Leptotyphlops carlae,* discovered in Barbados. Small enough to rest on a quarter and thin as shipping twine, the snake feasts on termite and ant larvae. The tiny snakes lay only one egg at a time... atypical for snakes, but necessary, as the egg can take up half of its mother's body.

Toothless Snake With Egg-Eating Vertebrae

The **EGG-EATING SNAKE,** a resident of southern Africa, has been given more than its fair share of oddities by Mother Nature. Although it doesn't posses venom—most species don't even have teeth!—it mimics its more dangerous brothers by rattling its scales together and striking aggressively. Its diet consists solely of unfertilized eggs, which it tests before eating. Once squeezed through the snake's elastic jaws, specialized vertebrae inside saw into the shell to extract the egg´s contents.

NEWS YOU CAN USE
Snakebite First-Aid

In the old days, people bit by snakes would often cut the wound and attempt to suck out the venom. This is not an effective method and can lead to infection. While there is no substitute for immediate care from a trained medical professional, keep these tips in mind when dealing with a snakebite:

    -call 911

    -from a safe distance, get a picture of the snake for ID

    -wash wound with soap and water

    -always keep the wound lower than the heart

    http://firstaid.about.com

Fastest Animals In Surf

Moving swiftly through water is no easy task, since it has a density almost 750 times that of air. Millions of years of evolution, however, have resulted in adaptations that make the most of the medium, leading to some truly swift creatures. The fastest of all ocean fish is the **SAILFISH**, which can reach speeds approaching 70 miles per hour in open water. Only the **SWORDFISH**, a fellow billfish, can claim to even approach the speeds of the sailfish. The **WAHOO** can hit almost 50 mph, but that is in the air when making a leap. The **FLYING FISH** can glide through the air at 35 mph, while the **ABALONE** is the fastest of the crawling creatures, moving at a rate of twelve-hundreths of a mile per hour.

Heart In Head

Next time you have some **SHRIMP** on the barbie, keep in mind just what a curious creature you are eating. The tiny aquatic creature's heart is located in its head! What's more, the tubular heart does not pump blood thoughout the body using a system of veins... rather, it dumps the blood directly into the animal's chest cavity, where it is absorbed by the internal organs. On second thought, maybe its better NOT to keep this in mind the next time you order shrimp!

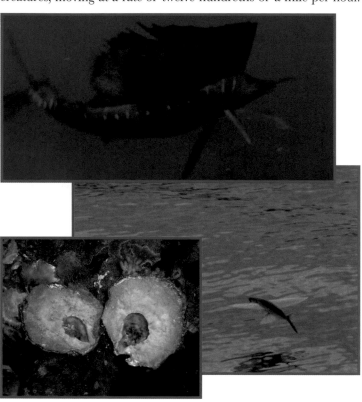

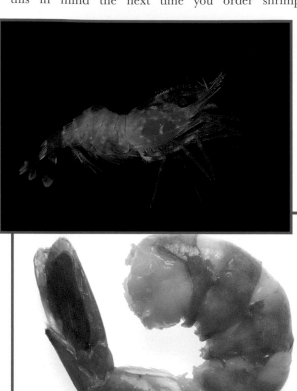

King Of Herring

In a sea brimming with curiosities, the **OARFISH** stands out. Also known as the ribbonfish or the King of Herring, the oarfish is a creature like no other. It is incredibly long and thin, spreading its 600-pound frame over an undulating, ribbon-like body that can stretch over fifty feet long! These denizens of the deep are only seen when they rise to the surface of the ocean when they are sick or dying, or when they wash up on a beach. It is thought that such occurances in antiquity gave rise to the fanciful tales of snake-like sea creatures so common in ancient texts.

Source: http://www.elasmo-research.org, http://www.science.edu.sg, http://www.seasky.org

Mimic Octopus...

Mother Nature has seen fit to give many animals an impressive array of venom and poision to protect themselves. But what happens when you don't have those defenses? One way to cope is give the appearance that you do... and none is better at that than the **MIMIC OCTOPUS** of Southeast Asia. This incredible creature can contort and reshape its pliable body to resemble an array of nasty creatues like the poisonous lion fish and flatfish. It can even bury all but two tentacles in the sand, leaving them free in the water to imitate a pair of deadly sea snakes!

..Colossal Calamari

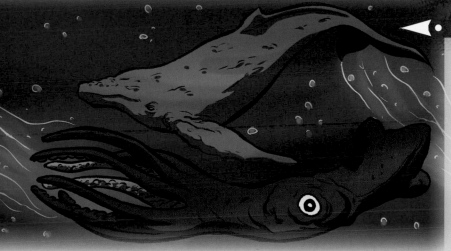

Squid are found all over the world, and come in all sizes. 300 species are known, but science suspects there may be many more that still remain undiscovered. Although differing greatly, they share some common characteristics, such as a hard shell under their mantle and three hearts in their bodies. The shallow-water species are marked by suction cups on their tentacles, while deep-water species sport large hooks. One such deep-water squid, the **COLOSSAL SQUID,** is the largest of them all, reaching a length of 35 feet and weighing in around the 1,000-pound mark. The eye of a giant squid is the same size as a basketball!

Deep Sea Dwellers....

Miles below the surface lies another world. In the depths, the water is extremely salty, almost freezing, under intense pressure, and pitch black. But many animals have adapted to the conditions and call this zone home. The **VAMPIRE SQUID** shares features of both squid and octupi, and swims using two large, ear-shaped flippers. Lacking ink or the ability to change color, it makes up for these deficiencies by having complete control over its bioluminescense. It uses its built-in light source for both defense and hunting. The **GIANT ISOPOD** looks like the land-based pillbug, except it can grow to a length of 16 inches! This sea-bottom scavenger will also make a meal out of sea cucumbers as well. And just like its terrestrial cousin, it rolls into a ball when threatened to protect its soft underbelly.

Source: http://www.nhm.ac.uk, http://www.squid-world.com, http://www.seasky.org

Deeply Ugly

The variety of life in the sea is amazing… and sometimes amazingly ugly! Take the **SEA CUCUMBER**—this slug-like, sausage-shaped animal lives on the sea floor and is often covered with spiky protrusions or warty bumps. Even more gross is its habit of shooting its guts out of its body when threatened, after which it simply grows more internal organs. The **BLOBFISH** of Australia is even more homely. To survive the great pressures of the sea floor, the fish forgoes muscles in favor of a body completetly composed of a gelatinous goo that is less dense than the seawater around it.

Transparent-Headed Fish

We've all made a comment about someone that seems to have eyes in the back of their head, but the tiny **BARRELEYE** fish does one better… it sees straight through its own transparent head! Living far down in the murky depths of the ocean, the barreleye is able to rotate its eyes upward, seeing through a special, transparent and liquid-filled shield that covers the top of its head. Once the barreleye has picked up a light source, such as bioluminescence from a jellyfish, it rotates its eyes back to forward position as it moves in for its meal.

Too Big For A Plate

Seafood is extremely popular with many people around the world, but spare a thought for the larger cousins of what appears on your plate. The **JAPANESE SPIDER CRAB'S** body isn't huge, but its legs sure are—they can reach a length of 13 feet! The crab's terrestrial cousin, the **COCONUT CRAB**, is the world's largest arthropod and is actually a type of hermit crab. It can grow to be over 3 feet long and weigh more than six and a half pounds. When it comes to shrimp, the most commonly eaten species around the world is the **BLACK TIGER SHRIMP**. Odds are you never ate one like the specimen found by a Colombian biologist in 2006, which was almost 16 inches long from tip to tail!

Source: http://www.itsnature.org, http://www.livescience.com, http://www.deepseamonsters.com, http://www.arkive.org, http://www.underwatertimes.com

More Teeth Than Mouth

When you think of toothy animals in the sea, the shark most readily pops to mind. But down in the inky depths lurks a fish with a mouth that has to be seen to be believed—the **VIPERFISH**. This long, thin-bodied fish terminates in a mouth filled with teeth so long and curved that the longest of them curl back toward the creature's eyes. It snags its prey by swimming full-speed into the victim, piercing it with its dagger-like teeth. To aid this attack, the first vertebra behind the viperfish's head acts as a shock absorber so it does not knock itself senseless while hunting. This fearsome fish is also phosphorescent and has a hinged skull to allow it to swallow very large prey.

Deadly Venom

The sea holds many dangers, and not all of the toothy variety. Far more deadly in many cases are the potent poisons of the blue ring octopus, box jellyfish, and beaked sea snake. The **BLUE RING OCTOPUS** may only be the size of a golf ball, but it contains venom strong enough to kill 26 adults! Those unfortunate enough to be bitten by the octopus have a slim chance of survival, as death can come in mere moments. The **BOX JELLYFISH** needs its strong venom to capture and kill shrimp, but humans can meet the same fate. Its tentacles adhere to the flesh once the sting is administered, and attempting to remove them will only worsen the sting and seal the victim's fate. Unlike the other two animals, the **BEAKED SEA SNAKE** is not at all passive. It has a reputation for agressive behavior, and its venom packs a punch 50 times stronger than any land-based snake.

Weird Sharks

Some varieties of shark, such as the great white, tiger, bull, and hammerhead, are well known to most people. But, as in every other species, nature has cooked up a whole host of strange variations on the shark theme. The **FRILLED SHARK**, mostly found in the deep waters off Japan, has a triangular, lizard-like head and tubular, eel-shaped body, with a mouth at the front of its head rather than underneath as in other sharks. The **GOBLIN SHARK** sports a bright pink skin over a soft, flabby body. Even more curious is its long, pointed snout, which is filled with electrosensitive organs used for prey detection. The **COOKIECUTTER SHARK** is a small, cigar-shaped specimen that produces a green bioluminescence. The shark's name comes from the neat, round plugs of flesh it removes from its victims after attaching itself to its prey using its lips as a tight seal before biting.

NEWS YOU CAN USE
Avoiding A Shark Attack

Sharks are one of the earth's oldest animals, found in waters all over the world. When you step in the ocean, you are stepping into shark country. Luckly, they rarely attack people. Keeping the following items in mind will further proctect you from becoming a snack: avoid wearing jewelry or objects that can flash in the sunlight; only swim in the day, as evening, night, and morning are shark feeding times; avoid murky water and rivermouths; avoid offshore channels or areas with a steep drop-off. If you spot a shark while in the water, swim calmly, without sudden movements, toward the beach or boat. Try to keep the shark in sight, as they seem to shy away when stared at.

Source: http://www.barrierreefaustralia.com, http://library.thinkquest.org, http://na.oceana.org, http://www.allthesea.com, http://www.elasmo-research.org

UNBREAKABLE

Fastest Air Animals

Birds are lords of the air, but did you know they are also the fastest animals on Earth? A **COMMON SWIFT**, for example, can hit speeds of 106 mph as it maneuvers through the air in search of a meal. No cheetah can match that! Even faster is the **PEREGRINE FALCON**, which can fly at 90 mph and hit 200 mph when in a dive. When hunting for smaller birds it smashes into its prey at high speed, knocking the victim out before circling back in mid-air to catch its meal before it plummets to earth.

Butt-Talking Caterpillars

Animals use many methods to communicate, but none is more bizarre than the habit of many **CATERPILLARS**—talking with their butts! When defending the silken shelter they construct on leaves, caterpillars of older evolutionary development simply try to bite and push, but the younger generations prefer to "argue." They use special oar-like structures on their rear ends to scrape and drum the leaf surface, sending a message to their rival that it is time to get lost!

NEWS YOU CAN USE

Avoiding A Bear Attack

You're face to face with a bear in the wild—it runs faster than you, can climb trees better than you, and can swim better than you. What do you do? **LET THE BEAR KNOW YOU ARE HUMAN**—make noise and wave your arms. **STAND YOUR GROUND** and don't run, or you'll trigger an attack. If you ARE attacked, **DO NOT RESIST**. Playing dead will remove you as a threat in the bear's eyes, and as long as you remain motionless you will be safe from attack. Once you are sure the bear is gone, proceed to safety as fast as possible!

Source: http://www.livescience.com, http://www.wisegeek.com, http://www.extremescience.com, http://www.fs.fed.us

Freaky Feathered Friends

The huge variety of life on Earth means that there are many strange and curious animals, and birds are certainly no exception. The **HOATZIN** of South America has an extremely small head and distinctive manure smell, resulting in it's nickname as the "stinkbird." New Zealand's **KIWI** is famously flightless, lacks a tail of any kind, and is one of the few birds that possesses a sense of smell. The **HOODED PITOHUI** of New Guinea is actually poisonous, with a neurotoxin found in its skin and feathers. Any animal touching the bird will experience a tingling sensation and numbness caused by the toxin.

Long Leapers

By far Australia's most famous animal, the kangaroo is well known for its leaping abilities: the large **RED KANGAROO** can jump 10 feet in the air and go 40 mph, while the **EASTERN GREY** can cover 29 feet in a single jump. Less well known is the fact that a kangaroo's back feet cannot move independently of each other, except when swimming. Kangaroos also lack the ability to move backward!

Kangaroo Attack

Although **KANGAROOS** are vegetarians and attacks are rare, they do occur. Kangaroo attacks are usually caused as a result of human interaction, when hand-fed roos are denied their expected snack. A male may also attack to protect his females. An aggressive roo will "sit" on its tail, freeing its strong back legs to deliver a devastating kick. Their strong claws can also deliver scratches and nasty puncture wounds. There has only been one human fatality due to roo attack, however, when a hunter was killed in 1936 while trying to protect his dogs from an enraged animal.

Source: http://www.weirdworm.com, http://www.kangaroofacts.net, http://www.amazingaustralia.com.au

Wolverine Tough

The **WOLVERINE** is legendary for its fierce nature, and roams the snowy wastes far from human habitation. The largest member of the weasel family, the wolverine's body is a mass of muscle that allows it to fight off threats from larger animals such as wolves and mountain lions, and sometimes even grizzly bears. It is an omnivore, with a diet ranging from roots and berries to rabbits and rodents, and even to scavanged meals from wolf kills. Most amazingly, the wolverine sometimes takes on large prey like caribou or elk, and will even dig through the snow to find and eat hibernating animals in winter.

Quake-Sensing Toads

The tales of animals predicting an earthquake before it happens are common, but are they backed up by science? Not really… until recently, anyway. Scientists monitoring a colony of common **TOADS** in Italy noticed that the toads suddenly and uncharacteristically abandoned their spawning grounds... and five days later an earthquake struck. The toads were somehow able to detect the pre-earthquake increase of radon levels or the shift in the earth's magnetic field with enough time to slowly make their way to safer grounds. It's possible other animals can detect quakes in similar fashion, but only toads have proven their powers of divination.

Earthwide Commute

The next time you're stuck in a car or bus cursing your daily commute, be glad you're not the **ARCTIC TERN**. This foot-long bird is the undisputed king of the commute, traveling from Greenland to Antarctica in its annual migration—an average distance of 44,000 miles! The birds fly south from Greenland until they split in western Africa, with half the flock heading directly south and the other half shadowing the South American coast, until they meet again in the cold Weddell Sea of Antarctica. They make the trip back together, going out of their way to hitch a ride on the high-speed jet stream winds.

Source: http://www.buzzle.com, http://www.livescience.com

Big Teeth

ELEPHANT tusks may look horn-like, but they are actually huge incisor teeth. In fact, a third of the tusk is actually buried out of sight in the animal's head. While all African elephants have tusks, only a portion of Asian male elephants have them. In both types of elephants, the tusks never stop growing, so an old animal can boast a huge set. The tusks are used as defense against lion attacks, to forage for food, or to battle other elephants to raise their status in the herd. Although poaching remains a problem, the world is united against the ivory trade to ensure these majestic animals have a secure future.

Speedy Tongue

The **GIANT ANTEATER** of South America has a very curious apperance, with a cone-shaped head which contains absolutely no teeth! It does possess a very useful tongue, however, which it uses to obtain its meal of ants and termites. Finding its prey by smell, the anteater tears into an anthill or termite nest with sharp claws, then flicks its tongue inside at a speed of 160 times a minute to extract the insects without getting bitten. Ever opportunistic, the anteater takes care never to destroy a nest, so it can return in the future for another meal.

Giant Butterfly

Papua New Guinea is an island nation north of Australia, filled with high mountains and thick jungles. It is also home to the world's largest winged insect, the **QUEEN ALEXANDRA BIRDWING BUTTERFLY.** The females of the species are larger than the males, and have a wingspan of up to 1 foot. They are seldom seen by man, as their short, 4-month lives are spent above the forest canopy, making them invisible from below. There they polinate plants, protected from bird attacks by strong toxins in their bodies and brightly colored wings that serve as a warning to other animals about their poisonous nature.

Source: http://www.eleaid.com, http://animals.nationalgeographic.com, http://www.extremescience.com

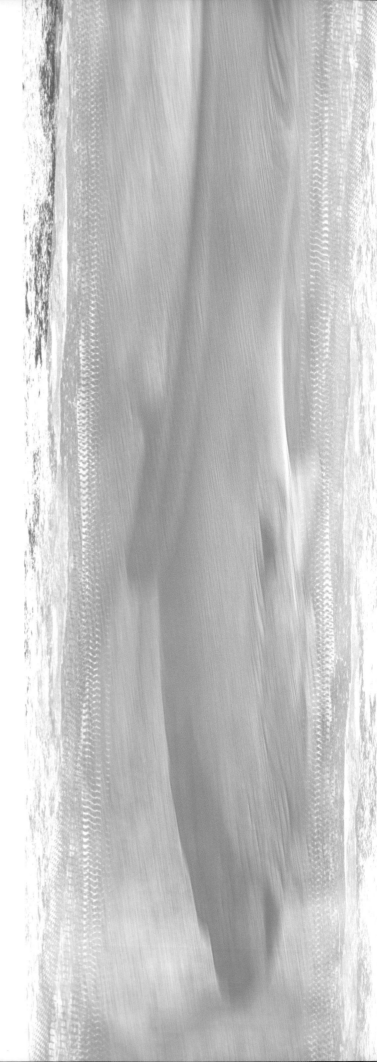

GET IN THE ACTION!

Why just read the **BOOK OF EXTREME FACTS** when you can be featured in it yourself? Perhaps this chapter has inspired you to set or share some records of your own, such as:

• Newly discovered wonders of the animal kingdom!
• Amazing feats performed by your own pet!
• Weird animal interactions, like cats riding goats!

Remember, you are not limited to the above suggestions, or to trying to beat other records in this chapter. Entirely new records are not only allowed… they are encouraged! The only limit is your own creativity. So have some fun (but always remember to keep it SAFE), and if you are younger than 18 remember to ask your parents for permission before attempting any record.

To submit a record:

-Go to *www.bookofextremefacts.com*

-Click on the "Submit New Record" tab

-Provide a brief description of your record and your contact info

-If we decide that your record makes the grade, we will contact you for further details and photos or video of your record

It's just that simple! Good luck…
and **KEEP IT EXTREME!**

Involvement in dangerous sports and related activities carries a significant risk of damage to property, personal injury or death. Please do not endanger yourself or others or take any unnecessary risks. If you choose to participate in dangerous sports or activities in attempting to achieve a distinction that would be recognized in the next edition of Extreme Facts, which IDW does not recommend, you do so at your own risk. IDW suggests the use of professional instruction before entering into any sports or physical activity. You should become knowledgeable about the risks involved. By submitting information to IDW related to inclusion in a future edition of Extreme Facts you assume personal responsibility for your actions and agree to indemnify and hold harmless IDW for the consequences of your actions.

IMAGE CREDITS

Page 73 - FASTEST ANIMALS ON TURF Ostrich Photo by MathKnight
Page 73 - FASTEST ANIMALS ON TURF Cockroach
        Photo by Joao Estevao A. de Freitas
Page 74 - RED SWEAT Photo by Nevit Dilmen
Page 75 - SNAKES IN THE AIR Photo by Conrad Baetsle
Page 76 - FASTEST ANIMALS IN SURF Photo by Richard Giddins
Page 79 - DEEPLY UGLY Photo by Cubanito
Page 79 - TOO BIG FOR A PLATE Photo by Hans Hillewaert
Page 80 - DEADLY VENOM Photo by Jens Petersen
Page 80 - WEIRD SHARKS Photo by OpenCage
Page 81 - BUTT-TALKING CATERPILLARS Photo by Daniel Schwen
Page 82 - LONG LEAPERS Photo by Quartl
Page 83 - QUAKE-SENSING TOADS Photo by Karamell
Page 84 - GIANT BUTTERFLY Photo by Mark Pellegrini

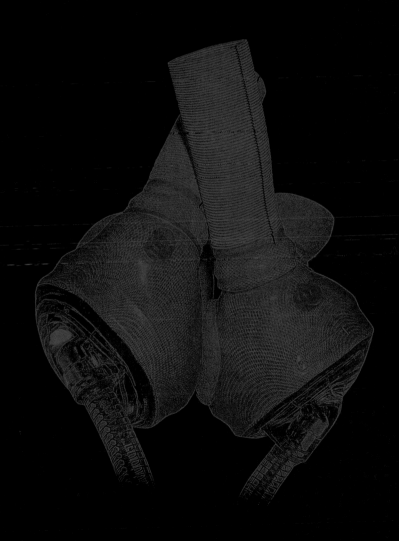

CHAPTER 6
MACHINES

The Fastest Car

The fastest production car in the world is the Bugatti Veyron, which goes from 0 to 60 in 2.5 seconds and tops out at 267 miles per hour. It starts with a **BASE PRICE OF $1.7 MILLION.** Its speed falls shy of breaking the record held by the jet-powered Thrust SSC that cracked 763 miles per hour back in 1997 and became the only car to ever break the sound barrier.

......The Fastest Gun

In December 2010, the U.S. Navy tested a new railgun that uses electromagnetic pulses to propel a projectile up to 100 miles away at **A SPEED OF UP TO MACH 7**. At 33 megajoules, its muzzle energy is triple that of any conventional gun, producing a blow roughly equal to 33 cars hitting a target at 100 miles per hour.

First Computer Game

THE FIRST COMPUTER TO EVER RUN A GAME was the EDSAC (Electronic Delay Storage Automatic Calculator), completed in 1949 by a team led by Sir Maurice Wilkes at the University of Cambridge in England. In 1952, A.S. Douglas designed an EDSAC program called OXO, which played Tic-Tac-Toe on an early computer monitor.

UNBREAKABLE

The Fastest Machine

The fastest vehicle ever made is NASA's X-43 Hyper-X scramjet. It topped out just shy of Mach 10—around **7,000 MILES PER HOUR**—during an unmanned test flight. The fastest piloted jet is still Lockheed's SR-71 Blackbird, which reached over 2,193 miles per hour back in 1976. The fastest machine ever was the Helios 2 solar probe. It hit over 150,000 miles per hour while in orbit.

Source: http://www.thesupercars.org, www.foxnews.com, http://www.computernostalgia.net, http://www.aerospaceweb.org

Biggest Bomb...

The largest nuclear weapon ever detonated was the Big Ivan, or the Tsar Bomba. A **100-MEGATON** Soviet device, it was scaled back to just over 50 to reduce nuclear fallout. During its only test, the bomb's mushroom cloud rose roughly 40 miles into the sky, and the blast was seen over 165 miles away. Everything within 15 miles of the detonation was utterly destroyed.

The Fastest Runner Without Legs

Japanese Vending Machines

In Japan, you can buy all sorts of things from the vending machines that line the streets. This includes soft drinks, vegetables, eggs, ties, umbrellas, sneakers, flowers, sake, cigarettes, beer, ice, books, manga, and more. The demand is so high that there's **ONE MACHINE FOR EVERY 23 PEOPLE** in the nation, and more are being installed all the time.

In 2008, the Olympics initially banned South African sprinter Oscar Pistorius from competing in that year's summer games. He is **A DOUBLE AMPUTEE** below the knee, and the Olympic Committee was concerned he was too good — that his prostheses gave him an unfair advantage over other runners. He was later reinstated and failed to qualify by only three-quarters of a second.

...The Difference Engine

Charles Babbage started work on a mechanical computer back in 1821, but he was unable to scrape together enough money to complete building it. Instead, the first computer based on his designs—Difference Engine No. 2—wasn't completed until 2002. It has **8,000 PARTS,** weighs 5 tons, and stands 7 feet high and 11 feet long. It works perfectly.

Source: http://www.nuclearweaponarchive.org, www.toxel.com, http://www.computerhistory.org, http://www.bbc.co.uk/news/

Gas Guzzlers

The car with the worst fuel efficiency is the **LAMBORGHINI MURCIELAGO**, which gets 8 miles to the gallon. It still beats the U.S. Army's M-1 Abrams tank, which requires 8 gallons to the mile. The F-14 fighter jet is even worse. It burns 14,400 gallons of fuel per hour.

First Microwaved Food

The principles behind the microwave oven were discovered by accident. Dr. Percy Spencer of the Raytheon Corporation was studying magnetrons—tubes that produce microwaves—for use in radar systems when he realized that the candy bar in his pocket had melted. He decided to try it on some food on purpose. The first thing he cooked? **POPCORN!**

The First TV Man

John Logie Baird demonstrated **THE FIRST TV** set in London in 1926 and broadcast images across the Atlantic to New York City in 1927. His mechanical device, which included a motorized spinning disk to capture and display scan lines on the screen, became obsolete when electronic TVs came along. Baird developed a means of recording TV on a disc and the first color TV, too.

Amphibious Roadster

The Watercar company builds the Python, the world's fastest amphibious vehicle. A convertible built on a Corvette powertrain, it can go from 0 to 60 in 4.5 seconds on land, and it can also do **OVER 60 MILES PER HOUR IN THE WATER,** fast enough for you to water ski behind it. Each is hand-built, and they start at $200,000 apiece.

Source: http://www.museum.tv, http://www.gallawa.com, http://www.envirosagainstwar.org, http://www.watercar.com

Largest Earth Mover

The largest movable machine in the world is the Bagger 288 Bucket Wheel Excavator built by ThyssenKrupp. It stands 30 stories tall, is over 700 feet long, and **WEIGHS 45,500 TONS**. It requires five people to operate it, and when traveling it moves at a top speed of about a third of a mile per hour. It's used in open-pit coal mines in Germany.

.......The Luke Arm

Dean Kamen, the inventor of the Segway, has invented a prosthetic arm named the Luke arm, after Luke Skywalker (who notably lost his arm to Darth Vader). Designed to help soldiers who lose arms during a war, it features a full range of movement and includes all five fingers on its hand, which has enough sensitivity that the user can even **EAT WITH CHOPSTICKS**.

The Flying Car

The Terrafugia company has developed and tested a flying car it hopes to put into production in 2011. It's a **TWO-SEATER PLANE** that can fold in its wings or extend them at the push of a button inside the cockpit. On land, it drives on four wheels, is street legal as a car, and can be parked in a garage.

Source: http://www.terrafugia.com, http://technologydigest.blogspot.com, http://medgadget.com

…Most Powerful Laser

The University of Texas-Austin currently has the most powerful active laser in the word, rated at **1.1 PETAWATTS.** That's about two thousand times as powerful as all the power plants in the U.S., although the laser is only used for tiny fractions of a second. Texas is also working on an Exawatt laser that's a thousand times more powerful than that.

A Bigger Ben

The world's largest clock started operation in 2010 in the city of Mecca in Saudi Arabia. It sits atop the nearly 1,900-foot tower of the Abraj Al Bait Towers, which will be the world's second tallest building when it's complete. Each of the clock's four faces is 151 feet wide, **SIX TIMES THE SIZE OF THE FACES ON BIG BEN,** and its lights can be seen up to 19 miles away.

Most Powerful Engine

The world's most powerful engine—a Wärtsilä RT-flex96C engine—is used to move a huge shipping freighter called the Emma Maersk. It's the first engine to use 14 cylinders. It weighs 2,500 tons, measures **90 FEET LONG AND 44 FEET WIDE,** and it generates 80,080 kilowatts.

NEWS YOU CAN USE

3D Printers

If you think printing your own photos or books at home is cool, wait until you get your hands on a 3D printer. These devices work by laying down thin layers of **A STRONG, QUICK-DRYING PLASTIC** to build an item. As long as you have the computerized plans, you can print all sorts of things—including the parts for another 3D printer!

Source: http://www.physorg.com, http://www.designboom.com, http://www.wartsila.com, http://reprap.org

The Astronomical Clock located at the Old Town Hall in the center of Prague shows the positions of the Sun and Moon and the constellations of the Zodiac on a massive three-layered dial. It was built in 1410, and it **STILL RUNS ON ITS ORIGINAL MECHANISM** to this day. Amazingly, it has no means of telling the actual hour.

WHO'S GOT NEXT?

ONE BIG BIKE

In 2007, 93 people got together in Germany to ride the world's longest tandem bike. For this feat, they cheated just a bit by using Kettwiesel tricycles, which can be attached to each other in a flexible chain as long as you care to make. All told, this bike stretched almost 500 **FEET LONG** and weighed about 3,200 pounds—and that's not even including the riders!

Big Bangs and Bells

The Tsar Cannon, built in Russia in 1586 with a caliber of 890 millimeters, is the largest cannon ever made. It fires **STONE CASE-SHOT,** or it would if it had ever actually been fired. Instead, it sits unused on display in the Kremlin, just around the corner from the 200-ton Tsar Bell, which cracked before it ever rang a single note.

Source: http://www.moscow-taxi.com, http://utf.mff.cuni.cz, http://hasebikes.com

Da Vinci's War Machines

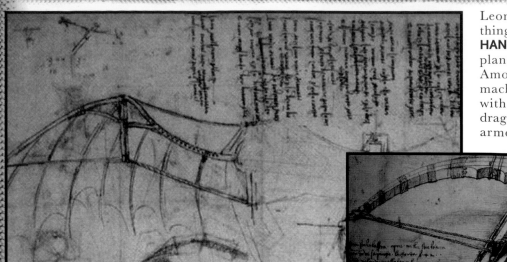

Leonardo Da Vinci designed many things before their time, **INCLUDING THE HANG GLIDER**. He also came up with plans for many different war machines. Among them were a 12-barreled machine cannon, a circular tank ringed with cannons, a horse-drawn chariot dragging a spinning set of blades, and an armored boat with a mounted cannon.

The Sharpest Water.

By pressurizing water to 60,000 pounds per square inch and spraying it through a tiny nozzle, you can make the stream **CUT THROUGH STEEL**, stone, glass, or just about anything shy of a diamond. They can make sharp, intricate cuts other machines can't manage and have even been used on things as soft as candy bars and diapers.

Early Aerial Combat

The first fighter pilots took to the skies during World War I. At the start of the war, pilots could **ONLY FIRE PISTOLS** from their open cockpits. Soon they mounted machine-guns on the front of their planes, but the trick was firing through a plane's propeller without hitting the blades. The Fokker company came up with a synchronization gear that allowed the pilot to do just that.

Source: http://dsc.discovery.com, http://waterjets.org, http://www.centennialofflight.gov

The Bionic Ear

The latest advancement in help for the deaf and hard of hearing is the cochlear implant. Doctors surgically implant a device behind the user's ear that bypasses the inner ear and stimulates the auditory nerve. It communicates with a microphone the user wears behind the ear. Nearly **190,000 PEOPLE IN THE WORLD HAVE THEM.**

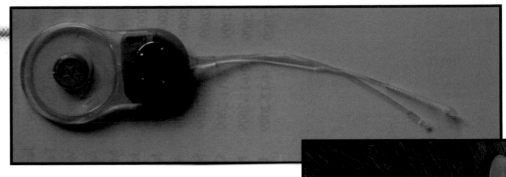

Have an (Artificial) Heart

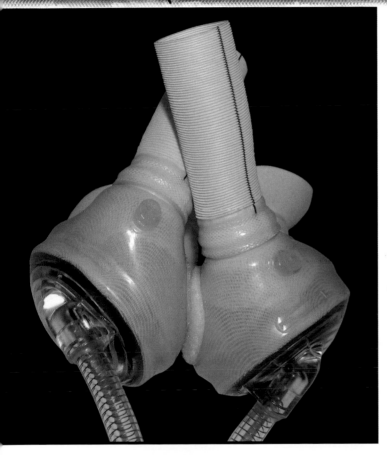

Charles Okeke is the first man to have an artificial heart implanted in his chest that doesn't require him to be stuck in a hospital and hooked up to a 400-pound machine to run and power it. Instead, he wears a battery-powered backpack that **ONLY ADDS 13 POUNDS** to his load and allowed him to go home and sleep in his own bed for the first time in years.

Big Bucks Machine

The record for the most money ever won from a slot machine is **$38.7 MILLION DOLLARS.** It happened at the Excalibur in Las Vegas back in 2003, through a progressive payout system that networked together slot machines in 157 casinos throughout Las Vegas. The winner had put in $3 for the winning pull on that one-armed bandit.

UNBREAKABLE

A Real Enigma

The Enigma machine was a tool the Nazis used in World War II to send unbreakable encrypted messages to each other. A number of successful missions aimed at capturing Enigma machines and their codes allowed the Allies to decipher Enigma messages without alerting the Germans and **HELPED END THE WAR EARLY.**

Source: http://www.nidcd.nih.gov, http://www.cbsnews.com, http://www.2worldwar2.com

The Franken-Cell

In the spring of 2010, scientists at the J. Craig Venter Institute announced that they'd successfully implanted an artificial set of DNA into a living cell, thereby **CREATING A NEW FORM OF LIFE.** They implanted it into a living bacteria cell, which it then took over from the inside. It later managed to replicate all by itself.

Fastest Machine-Gun

The world's fastest machine-gun is a prototype nicknamed "Bertha" and built by Mike O'Dwyer of Metal Storm. It uses an electric current to fire the bullets, which are stacked behind each other in each of its 36 barrels, and it fires 180 bullets in less than a hundredth of a second. That's a rate of **OVER 1 MILLION A MINUTE.**

A Soldier's Best Friend

The BigDog robot developed by Boston Dynamics is a four-legged walking platform that stands 2.5 feet tall and 3 feet long and weighs 240 pounds. It moves at 4 miles an hour, a steady walking pace, and can carry up to 350 pounds of gear through rough terrain. It's meant to **HELP SOLDIERS TRANSPORT GEAR** into otherwise inaccessible areas.

Source: http://online.wsj.com, http://tvtropes.org, http://www.bostondynamics.com

Not Quite Human

Honda produces the most versatile robot in the world, ASIMO. **IT'S BUILT LIKE A HUMAN,** and it stands about 4' 3" tall and weighs 120 pounds. It can move at over 3.5 miles per hour and can open doors, switch on lights, recognize people's faces, recognize and obey gestures and voice commands, carry a tray, push a cart, and guide people through buildings.

Squeeze Water from Air

Aqua Sciences makes machines that gather moisture from the air and turn it into drinking water. Their biggest equipment can create 1,250 gallons of water a day at a cost of roughly a quarter per gallon. In areas in which there's no access to clean drinking water, this can be **A REAL LIFE SAVER!**

Flying Submarine....

The Pentagon is also trying to develop **A FLYING SUBMARINE—** a vehicle that can travel deep under and high over the waves. They hope to manage it by using new submersible technology that puts wings on submarines and allows them to "fly" underwater by angling the wings so that forward thrust pushes the craft down.

Source: http://world.honda.com, http://www.newscientist.com, http://www.aquasciences.com

Fastest Camera...

Researchers at UCLA have created the world's fastest camera. Using lasers to capture the images—rather than capturing light like a traditional camera—it can grab **6.1 MILLION SHOTS IN A SINGLE SECOND.** If you played that back at the standard 24 frames per second of a film, it would take more than 70 hours to watch a second's worth of photos.

...Commute by Jet Pack

Today, you can purchase your own jet pack—technically a rocket belt—and fly for about a half a minute on your own. Jet Belt International soon plans to release its new **JET PACK T-73,** which lets you cruise for 9 full minutes at over 80 miles per hour.

Big TVs

When the Dallas Cowboys opened their new stadium in 2008, the teams started playing under the largest video screens in the world. The two longer displays measure **160 FEET LONG BY 72 FEET TALL,** and along with the ones that face the end zones they total 600 tons. Each has 10.5 million LED bulbs and provides a full HD (1080p) picture.

Source: http://blogs.discovermagazine.com, http://www.jetpackinternational.com, http://stadium.dallascowboys.com

GET IN THE ACTION!

Why just read the **BOOK OF EXTREME FACTS** when you can be featured in it yourself? Perhaps this chapter has inspired you to set or share some records of your own, such as:

• Homemade inventions that have to be seen to be believed!
• Labor-saving devices propelling us into the future!
• Modified cars, bikes, or vehicles that are utterly unique!

Remember, you are not limited to the above suggestions, or to trying to beat other records in this chapter. Entirely new records are not only allowed… they are encouraged! The only limit is your own creativity. So have some fun (but always remember to keep it SAFE), and if you are younger than 18 remember to ask your parents for permission before attempting any record.

To submit a record:

-Go to www.bookofextremefacts.com

-Click on the "Submit New Record" tab

-Provide a brief description of your record and your contact info

-If we decide that your record makes the grade, we will contact you for further details and photos or video of your record

It's just that simple! Good luck…
and **KEEP IT EXTREME!**

Involvement in dangerous sports and related activities carries a significant risk of damage to property, personal injury or death. Please do not endanger yourself or others or take any unnecessary risks. If you choose to participate in dangerous sports or activities in attempting to achieve a distinction that would be recognized in the next edition of Extreme Facts, which IDW does not recommend, you do so at your own risk. IDW suggests the use of professional instruction before entering into any sports or physical activity. You should become knowledgeable about the risks involved. By submitting information to IDW related to inclusion in a future edition of Extreme Facts you assume personal responsibility for your actions and agree to indemnify and hold harmless IDW for the consequences of your actions.

IMAGE CREDITS

Page 86 - THE FASTEST CAR Photo by Xavigivax
Page 87 - THE FASTEST RUNNER WITHOUT LEGS Photo by Elvar Pálsson
Page 87 - JAPANESE VENDING MACHINES Photo by Wm Jas
Page 88 - GAS GUZZLERS Photo by Jordan Walker
Page 88 - FIRST MICROWAVED FOOD Photo by Bunchofgrapes
Page 89 - LARGEST EARTH MOVER Photo by Martinroell
Page 91 - THE ASTRONOMICAL CLOCK Photo by Clock
Page 91 - ONE BIG BIKE Photo by Drahkrub
Page 93 - THE BIONIC EAR Photo by Edwtie
Page 93 - HAVE AN (ARTIFICIAL) HEART Photo by JNakashima
Page 93 - BIG BUCKS MACHINE Photo by Josh Truelson
Page 97 - BIG TVs Photo by Klobetime

CHAPTER 7

SCIENCE

........Spider-Goats!

Geneticists at the University of Wyoming have **GENETICALLY COMBINED SPIDERS AND GOATS** to create goats that produce a milk filled with the proteins found in spider silk. They hope to then refine the milk to create large quantities of this silk, which is incredibly strong, to make sutures for wounds that are otherwise hard to treat.

Moving Fast And Hard

A proton zipping through the Large Hadron Collider gets up to a speed that is just shy of the **SPEED OF LIGHT**. Because of this, even though the proton is so small, it has roughly the kinetic energy of a small car moving at over 1,000 miles per hour. When two of them collide, the head-on collision is spectacular.

....Men Or Mice?

To test the promise of human embryonic stem-cell research, scientists injected such cells into the brains of mice still in their mothers' wombs. Amazingly, a small percentage of the stem cells survived and transformed into **HUMAN BRAIN CELLS WORKING INSIDE OF THE BRAINS OF THE MICE!**

Source: http://www.nsf.gov, http://lhc.web.cern.ch, http://www.washingtonpost.com

Natural Reactors

In Gabon, a small state in Africa, uranium deposits once formed a natural nuclear reactor that kicked out 15 gigawatt-years of energy during a period around two billion years ago. Fortunately, a nearby river cooled the core and **KEPT IT FROM EXPLODING.**

The First A-Bomb

The first atomic bomb blast took place on July 16, 1945, in New Mexico. The scientists who built it were so confident (or at least hopeful) that it would work that they shipped another bomb out to the U.S. forces in the Pacific for use on Hiroshima on August 6, **JUST THREE WEEKS LATER.**

Watching Nukes From Vegas

In the 1950s, the U.S. Government regularly tested nuclear bombs in an area 65 miles northwest of Las Vegas. **CASINOS USED THIS AS A TOURIST ATTRACTION** and set up events during which people could watch the blasts from the upper levels of the tallest hotels. Those who wanted to get closer could picnic at the edge of the government land.

NEWS YOU CAN USE

The Candy that Glows in the Dark

When you bite into a piece of sugary candy, you trigger something called **TRIBOLUMINESCENCE**. When you crush the sugar molecules, they emit a spark of ultraviolet light. You can't normally see this, but if you try it with a candy made with naturally luminescent wintergreen, it will slow the frequency of the spark down enough for you to see it.

Source: http://www.aip.org, http://www.eyewitnesstohistory.com, http://www.pbs.org, http://recipes.howstuffworks.com

That's Deep!

The device made on Earth that has traveled farther away from the planet than any other is the deep-space probe Voyager I, launched on September 5, 1979. As of 2010, it is **OVER 10 BILLION MILES AWAY** from home. It passed the previous record holder, Pioneer 10, in 1998. It carries an onboard record that contains various sounds and greetings from around the world—but instead of vinyl, this record is made of copper plated with gold!

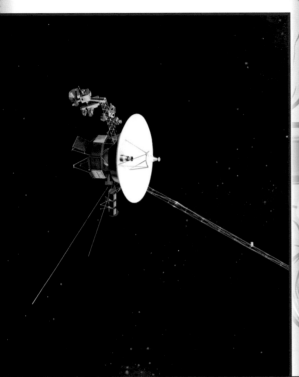

Grow Your Own Organs

At Wake Forest University, researchers have come up with a way to **GROW AN ENTIRELY NEW HUMAN BLADDER IN A LAB** from a patient's own cells. It can then be transplanted in place of a bad bladder and give full function without chance of rejection. They hope to use this procedure to grow other organs soon.

The Longest Time On Mars

The Mars rover Opportunity is the longest continuously running machine ever put on the Red Planet. It and its sister machine Spirit were **ONLY DESIGNED TO WORK FOR 90 DAYS,** but Opportunity broke the record of six years and 116 days in early 2010. Communications were lost with Spirit before it broke the record, but NASA scientists still hope to someday reestablish the link

The People Code

The Human Genome Project successfully identified **ALL 25,000 OR SO GENES IN HUMAN DNA** and even figured out the sequencing of the three billion chemical base pairs that make up those genes. The project required 13 years and over 200 principal investigators from at least 18 different countries. It was completed in 2003.

Source: http://msnbc.msn.com, http://voyager.jpl.nasa.gov, http://marsrover.nasa.gov, http://www.ornl.gov

I Spy From Orbit

The Hubble Space Telescope has been sending spectacular images of objects in space back to Earth for over 20 years. It is set to be replaced by the **JAMES WEBB SPACE TELESCOPE** in 2014. The Webb sees infrared light, allowing us to peer at the most distant things that we have ever seen.

Moon Call

Only a dozen people have ever set foot on the moon. They all did so in the course of just less than 29 months, between July 20, 1969, and December 17, 1972. They were all American men, astronauts flying for NASA, and **NO ONE FROM ANY OTHER COUNTRY HAS EVER REPEATED THE FEAT.**

Last Person On The Moon

The last human being on the moon was **AMERICAN CAPTAIN EUGENE CEMAN**. He flew into space three times but never returned to the moon's surface after the Apollo 17 mission that brought him there and back. The lunar module he landed in was nicknamed "Snoopy." The crew of Apollo 17 left the moon on December 17, 1972, and no one has been back to visit since.

Source: http://webbtelescope.org, http://www.nasa.gov, http://marklarson.com

Real-Life Tomb Raider

One of the greatest explorers of his age, **ROY CHAPMAN ANDREWS** brought the first motorized vehicles into the Gobi Desert, where he found the first fossils of dinosaur eggs as well as the fossils of other dinosaurs and some early mammals that lived beside them. He's reported to be one of the inspirations for Indiana Jones.

Finding The Titanic

Explorer **ROBERT BALLARD** has led over 120 deep-sea exploration missions, including the one that located the long-missing Titanic. Using the deep-sea submarine Alvin, he and his team discovered the wreck in 1986, sitting 12,460 feet below the surface of the icy North Atlantic Ocean. Ballard later led expeditions that found the Lusitania, the Bismarck, and President Kennedy's lost WWII patrol boat PT-109.

Supercroc!......

In 1990, an expedition led by explorer Paul Sereno discovered the fossils of **A PREHISTORIC SUPERCROC,** Sarcosuchus imperator. This creature stretched about 40 feet long—twice as long as any modern crocodile—and was powerful enough to eat other dinosaurs. It's estimated to have weighed around 17,500 pounds.

Source: http://www.roychapmanandrewssociety.org, http://www.titanic-titanic.com, http://www.supercroc.org

They Look Like Ants From Up Here

According to explorer Mark Moffett—a.k.a. Doctor Bugs—a single 2.5-acre plot of jungle floor contains **MORE THAN 8 MILLION ANTS**—that's more than the human population of New York City. And more than twice that number live in the trees above the ground as well.

UNBREAKABLE

Deep-Sea Diva

In 1979, explorer Sylvia Earle walked untethered on the ocean floor at a depth of 1,250 feet below the surface, setting a record that stands to this day. She also holds the solo dive depth record, having reached **3,300 FEET BELOW SEA LEVEL.** Today she leads the team adding maps of the world's oceans to Google Earth.

Real Zombies!

Ethnobotanist and explorer Wade Davis theorizes that Haitian priests create **ZOMBIES OF LIVING PEOPLE** by using tetrodotoxin, a naturally occurring neurotoxin found in certain types of fish, including the pufferfish. Combined with the force of the voodoo religion native to Haiti, this causes affected believers to come out of their coma in a trancelike state and behave like zombies.

Remote-Controlled Flying Beetles

Scientists at the University of California have implanted a microchip into a giant flower beetle and can control it by means of a remote signal sent by a laptop. With this, they can **MAKE THE BEETLE FLY, TURN, HOVER, AND LAND.** The U.S. Department of Defense hopes to use this technology for spying and for rescue missions.

Source: http://www.nybooks.com, The Serpent and the Rainbow by Wade Davis, http://www.nationalgeographic.com, http://www.technologyreview.com

The Oldest Humans

The earliest remains of humans yet discovered were found in Ethiopia. They date back 195,000 years. The earliest remains of an ancestor of humanity—Ardipithecus ramidus—were found in the same region. The name of this proto-human is Ardi, and **SHE LIVED 4.4 MILLION YEARS AGO.**

The Dwarf Planet

In 2006, the International Astronomical Union came up with a new definition of a planet that left Pluto outside of the family. Instead, it's now known as a dwarf planet, and it even comes in second place in that race behind the larger Eris. Recently, the term *dwarf planet* was dropped in favor of the term **PLUTOID**, giving our former 9th planet just a bit more respect.

Moon Smasher!

In 2009, NASA flew its LCROSS satellite **STRAIGHT INTO THE MOON.** The machine smashed into the surface, sending dust and debris high into the air. Upon analyzing this material, NASA discovered water in the forms of both ice and vapor. This confirmed the theory that there is water on the moon, something that future missions might be able to exploit while there.

Source: http://www.nationalgeographic.com, http://www.space.com, http://lcross.arc.nasa.gov

◄...Older Than The Stars

Scientists estimate that **THE UNIVERSE IS 13.7 BILLION YEARS OLD.** They narrowed this down from a range of 12 to 14 billion years by using data gathered by the WMAP Observatory, which takes six months to gather data from the entire sky—or as much of it as can be seen while orbiting the Earth.

Looking Back Into The Stars

In 2009, the Hubble Space Telescope took pictures of what are believed to be **THE MOST DISTANT GALAXIES EVER DISCOVERED.** Taking the photo required gathering light for 48 hours, and the picture shows light from stars that was emitted 13 billion years ago, less than a billion years after the universe began.

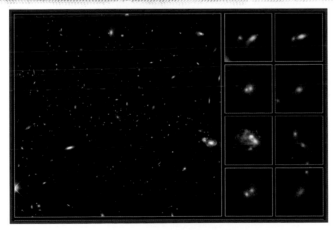

Strange New Planets

In 1995, scientists first discovered evidence of planets orbiting distant suns, starting with the giant orbiting **51 PEGASI.** Until 2009, about 400 had been confirmed, but with the launch of NASA's Kepler mission, we already have discovered signs of another 700 or so stars with some number of planets likely orbiting them.

NEWS YOU CAN USE

Reworking the Red Planet

Mars is the planet most like Earth in the entire Solar System. This means that it should be the easiest to transform into a planet on which humans can live, a process known as **TERRAFORMING.** One way to get started would be to induce global warming on Mars, something we're already learning a lot about on Earth.

Source: http://opa.yale.edu, http://map.gsfc.nasa.gov, http://www.planetary.org, http://quest.nasa.gov

Fly by Phone...

Parrot makes a 1-square-foot, four-rotor **QUADRICOPTER** that you can control with an iPhone. Better yet, the A.R. Drone has two cameras—one up front and one below—that you can see through on the iPhone, too. It can be used for alternate reality games and even midair dogfights!

Really Buggy...

THE FIRST COMPUTER BUG WAS A MOTH found trapped in a relay in an early computer used at Harvard University in 1945. The term "bug" had been used for decades before that to refer to many different kinds of technical problems. However, removing the moth was called "debugging," a term that sticks with computer programmers to this day.

The Skin Printer

Medical scientists at Wake Forest University have developed a machine that can actually **PRINT ARTIFICIAL SKIN GRAFTS DIRECTLY ONTO BURN VICTIMS.** The new skin is made from living tissue mixed with other ingredients, and it makes healing from such wounds much faster. No word on whether it can be used to cover up bad tattoos.

The Fastest Submarine...

The U.S. Navy is working on a new type of submarine that can **MOVE UNDERWATER AT UP TO 100 KNOTS** (about 115 miles per hour)—three or four times faster than current military subs can move. It uses a phenomena called supercavitation, which causes an air bubble to form around something that moves fast enough through water.

Source: http://www.popsci.com, http://ardrone.parrot.com, http://www.history.navy.mil, http://medgadget.com

The First Network

THE FIRST COMPUTER NETWORK of any kind was built in 1940 by George Stibitz of Bell Labs. Using a telegraph, he was able to access a computer in New York City while attending a conference at Dartmouth College. He could then use the remote machine to help solve difficult mathematical problems. World of Warcraft never entered his mind.

The Age Of The Internet

The direct predecessor of the Internet—**ARPAnet,** which was created by teams at MIT and the U.S. Department of Defense— started out in 1969, linking four universities in the western United States. In January 1983, ARPAnet switched its communications protocol to TCP/IP, the same system that we still use today.

The Largest Creature On Earth

The largest organism on the planet is not, as you might guess, the blue whale but instead **A PHENOMENAL FUNGUS GROWING UNDERNEATH OREGON.** This particular Armillaria ostoyae— a kind of honey mushroom—stretches up to four square miles and may be up to 8,650 years old. The first such monster mushroom was found in the Upper Peninsula of Michigan in 1992, but the new one in Oregon is much larger.

Source: http://www.computer.org, http://som.csudh.edu, http://www.scientificamerican.com

Arsenic And New Cells

In December 2010, NASA scientists revealed that they have discovered **A NEW FORM OF LIFE THAT USES ARSENIC**—which is poisonous to us—in place of the phosphorous found in almost every other living creature. This opens up the possibility of all sorts of new kinds of life that we never could have guessed at before.

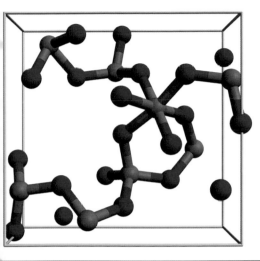

...The Vegetarian Robot

Engineers at Robotic Technology Incorporated have developed a robot that can **ACQUIRE AND DIGEST PLANTS** to provide itself the energy it needs to run. It's designed to be rugged enough to provide U.S. military troops with support, carrying their packs and even rescuing injured soldiers. RTI promises that the machine is strictly vegetarian.

Truly Super Glue

Doctors have figured out how to use medical-grade super glue to close open wounds, reducing the amount of scarring for some injuries that used to require stitches. Recently, they've been able to use it to **REPAIR BRAIN ANEURISMS** that would have otherwise proven fatal.

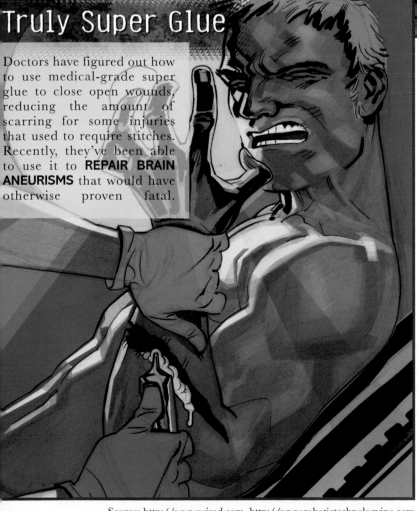

UNBREAKABLE

Atomic Microscopes

Electron microscopes can see things far smaller than any light-based microscope could hope to focus in on. A new breed of instruments called **ATOMIC FORCE MICROSCOPES** can zoom in even farther, about 1,000 times better than any light-based microscope could manage. They work by feeling the force between atoms and can show the shape of a strand of DNA or even the surface of an atom.

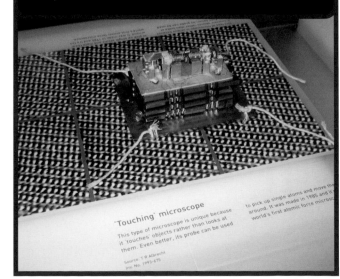

'Touching' microscope
This type of microscope is unique because it 'touches' objects rather than looks at them. Even better, its probe can be used to pick up single atoms and move them around. It was made in 1985 and it is the world's first atomic force microscope.

Source: T R Albrecht
Inv. No. 1993-475

Source: http://www.wired.com, http://www.robotictechnologyinc.com, http://www.dailymail.co.uk, http://www.nanooze.org

Send In The Clones

Scientists have been cloning animals for years, starting with a tadpole cloned in 1952. The first mammal successfully cloned was **A SHEEP NAMED DOLLY,** in 1997. Since then all sorts of mammals have been cloned, including an endangered wild ox and an endangered wild sheep. Current techniques fail about 98% of the time, so it's still extremely rare.

Five Liquid Metals

While mercury is the best-known liquid metal, all metals can melt if you get them hot enough. A total of five can become liquid on nothing more than a summer's day in Arizona. **CAESIUM, FRANCIUM, AND GALLIUM CAN ACTUALLY MELT IN YOUR HAND,** while rubidium melts at 102° F. Don't try this at home, though, as some of the metals can harm humans on contact.

Two Liquid Elements

Only two elements are liquid at room temperature. The obvious one is mercury, which can be found in thermometers around the world. The other is bromine, a red-brown material that causes sores on contact with skin. It's used in film developing and flame retardants, and **ITS FUMES CAN BE LETHAL.**

The First Hard Disk

IBM invented the first hard disk for use with a computer, and it was a monster! It could contain up to 5 megabytes of data, but to manage that it used 50 disks, each of which was two feet wide. It wasn't available for sale separately but only as part of the 305 RAMAC, which IBM leased to companies for **$3,200 PER MONTH!**

Tiny Robots

Scientists at New York University have built a **MICROSCOPIC ROBOT ENTIRELY OUT OF DNA.** It walks on two legs, each only 10 nanometers long. Researchers hope to figure out how to get it to move things as small as an atom and build things smaller than the human eye can see.

Source: http://www.ornl.gov, http://antoine.frostburg.edu, http://periodic.lanl.gov, http://gizmodo.com, http://www.sciencecentral.com

The First Mobile Phones

THE FIRST MOBILE PHONE WAS USED IN 1946 as part of an 80-pound system integrated into a car and used regular radio waves. It wasn't until 1983 that Illinois Bell set up the first commercial cell phone service. These phones weighed a pound and cost $3,500 each.

Printing Food

A team of scientists at Cornell University has come up with **A MACHINE THAT PRINTS FOOD** by using a set of computer-controlled syringes filled with liquid food inks. With it, anyone can create perfect food from recipes downloaded from gourmet chefs, and every piece can be designed to best suit the tastes and health or dietary needs of each diner at a table.

NEWS YOU CAN USE

Take a Nap

Research shows that a lack of sleep can harm the way the brain naturally processes short-term memories into long-term memories. Getting a little extra sleep in the form of a nap can also help you become more creative. To manage this, though, **THE NAP HAS TO BE WELL OVER AN HOUR**, enough to send you into the dreamland of REM.

Brain-Controlled Artificial Arms

Today, people who have lost an arm can have **A MODERN PROSTHETIC** attached. Through the use of electrodes placed on key parts of the body, the user can actually manipulate the prosthetic by nothing more than thinking about it. While the arms cannot move as well as an original limb, scientists are working on improving them every day.

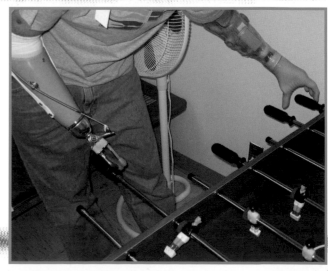

Source: http://www.corp.att.com, http://www.bbc.co.uk, http://www.nytimes.com, http://www.sciencecentral.com

GET IN THE ACTION!

Why just read the **BOOK OF EXTREME FACTS** when you can be featured in it yourself? Perhaps this chapter has inspired you to set or share some records of your own, such as:

• Fun and unique experiments that are NEWS YOU CAN USE!
• New knowledge about our world and universe discovered in your area!
• Out-of-this-world astronomical discoveries and phenomena!

Remember, you are not limited to the above suggestions, or to trying to beat other records in this chapter. Entirely new records are not only allowed... they are encouraged! The only limit is your own creativity. So have some fun (but always remember to keep it SAFE), and if you are younger than 18 remember to ask your parents for permission before attempting any record.

To submit a record:

-Go to *www.bookofextremefacts.com*

-Click on the "Submit New Record" tab

-Provide a brief description of your record and your contact info

-If we decide that your record makes the grade, we will contact you for further details and photos or video of your record

It's just that simple! Good luck…
and **KEEP IT EXTREME!**

Involvement in dangerous sports and related activities carries a significant risk of damage to property, personal injury or death. Please do not endanger yourself or others or take any unnecessary risks. If you choose to participate in dangerous sports or activities in attempting to achieve a distinction that would be recognized in the next edition of Extreme Facts, which IDW does not recommend, you do so at your own risk. IDW suggests the use of professional instruction before entering into any sports or physical activity. You should become knowledgeable about the risks involved. By submitting information to IDW related to inclusion in a future edition of Extreme Facts you assume personal responsibility for your actions and agree to indemnify and hold harmless IDW for the consequences of your actions.

IMAGE CREDITS

Page 104 - FINDING THE TITANIC Photo by Erik Charlton
Page 105 - THEY LOOK LIKE ANTS FROM UP HERE
            Photo by Smartse
Page 107 - STRANGE NEW PLANETS Photo by Debivort
Page 109 - ATOMIC MICROSCOPES Photo by John Dalton
Page 110 - FIVE LIQUID METALS Photo by Foobars
Page 110 - TWO LIQUID ELEMENTS Photo by Jurii
Page 110 - THE FIRST HARD DISK Photo by Mikaël Restoux

CHAPTER 8
EXTREME PEOPLE

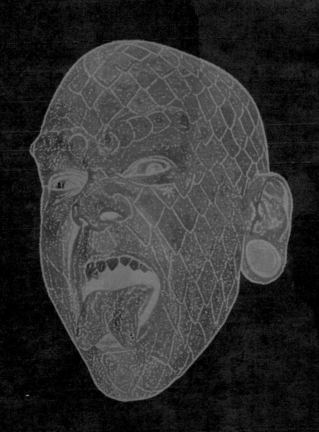

The Escape Artist

Harry Houdini was known far and wide as the handcuff king. He never found a set of handcuffs or a jail cell that could hold him. He even managed to break out of the Siberian Transport in Russia, a **STEEL-LINED PRISON ON WHEELS** that was built for transporting prisoners to the farthest reaches of that nation.

Most Total Piercings

The person who has the most body piercings in the world is Elaine Davidson. When she was first named the person with the most piercings in 2001, she had 462. As of April 2010, she had **6,925 PERMANENT PIERCINGS.** She estimates that the total weight of the metal attached to her is more than 6.5 pounds, but she claims she's comfortable even when sleeping.

UNBREAKABLE

Most Tattoos

The most tattooed person in the world is Lucky Diamond Rich, who has had every bit of his skin tattooed, including the inside of his mouth and his ears. He's spent over **1,100 HOURS** under the tattoo needle, and now that he's been covered entirely with blue-black ink, he's having another layer of patterns inked on him in white.

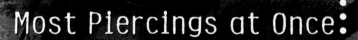

Most Piercings at Once:

In 2010, Ed Bruns broke the record for the most piercings of his body in a single session. In just under four and a half hours, he had **1,501 NEEDLES** inserted through his skin, turning him into a human pincushion. Right after that, all of the needles were removed. The hole from needle 1501 still sits in the back of his head with a tiny barbell through it.

Source: The Secret Life of Houdini: The Making of America's First Superhero by William Kalush and Larry Sloman, http://www.elainedavidson.co.uk, http://www.cbsnews.com, http://www.articlesbase.com

The Oldest Person Ever

Jeanne Calment of Arles, France, was born in 1875 and died in 1997 at the **TENDER AGE OF 122**. When she was 90, she sold her apartment to a lawyer on a contingency contract that required him to pay her every month and let her live in the apartment until she died. He died a year before she did.

Youngest College Graduate

Michael Kearny began speaking at 4 months old. He entered college at the age of 6 and graduated from the University of South Alabama **WHEN HE WAS 10,** making him the youngest college graduate ever. As an adult, he won $1 million dollars on the game show *Gold Rush.*

Day November 10, 2006
PAY TO THE ORDER OF:
Michael Kearney $1.000.000.00
One Million _____ Dollar

The Highest IQ

Although it's hard to measure intelligence well, Marilyn vos Savant, who writes the nationally syndicated column "Ask Marilyn" for *Parade* magazine has the **HIGHEST ESTIMATED IQ EVER RECORDED, AT 228.** She surrounds herself with smart people, too. Her husband, Robert Jarvik, invented the Jarvik artificial heart, and she serves as the Chief Financial Officer of his company.

...The Sixth Sense

Steve Haworth of Phoenix, Arizona, made his mark as a body modification artist, but he also came up with a method of implanting a powerful neodymium magnet in a person's body—usually on the side of the ring finger—so that you can actually **FEEL MAGNETIC FIELDS** as you near them, adding a sixth sense!

···Longest Hiccups

Charles Osborne holds the record for the longest bout of hiccups ever. He started in 1922 after a fall caused a tiny blood vessel to burst in his brain, destroying the part that suppresses hiccups. He kept hiccupping for **68 YEARS**, finally stopping the year before he died.

OCTOBER 5
Happy Birthday

Birthdays Common and Rare

Do you know a lot of people that share your birthday, or hardly anyone at all? The most common birthday in the U.S. is **OCTOBER 5th**, so if you celebrate then you have a lot of company. But if you are born on **MAY 22nd**, then you are a rare specimen, because that is America's least common birthday.

Lots of Babies

The largest number of babies ever born to any woman at once was nine, but none of the children have ever survived. Nadya Suleman of southern California gave birth to eight babies **(OCTUPLETS)** at once in 2009, and every one of them survived. They had six siblings waiting to welcome them home.

Source: http://anybirthday.com, http://topics.nytimes.com, http://www.people.com

The Most Stunts Pulled

Hong Kong actor **JACKIE CHAN** has performed more dangerous stunts in his long film career than any other actor. He used to handle all his own stunts, but he's now known to use doubles sometimes because no company will insure him. He's broken countless bones, but he refuses to quit working the way he knows best.

The Biggest Weight Loser

The heaviest man ever was Jon Brower Minnoch, who weighed about 1,400 pounds at his peak. (That put him as the second heaviest person behind Carol Yager, who weighed up to 1,600 pounds.) He once made it down from that point to 476 pounds. No one else has ever lost so much: about **974 POUNDS.**

The Loudest Scream

The person with the loudest scream ever measured is Jill Drake of England. She set the record at a screaming competition in 2000, hitting **AN EAR-SPLITTING 129 DECIBELS.** Serious pain starts to set in at 125 decibels, which is about as loud as an ambulance's siren.

Source: http://web.archive.org, http://www.dimensionsmagazine.com, http://news.bbc.co.uk

Longest Hair

Xie Qiuping of China holds the official record with his hair being measured at more than 18 feet long in 2004. However, the person with the world's longest hair was Tran Van Hay of Vietnam. At the time of his death in 2010, his hair supposedly measured more than **22 FEET AND 3 INCHES** from his scalp to its tip.

The Largest Gathering of People

The largest peaceful gathering of people ever occurred in India over the course of the 45-day-long Ardh Kuhbm Mela, a holy festival that's held every 12 years. The last time it took place, in 2007, an estimated **60 TO 70 MILLION PEOPLE** came to the spot where the Ganges and Yamuna Rivers run together to wash away their sins.

Longest Beard

The man with the longest beard ever recorded is Hans Langeth of North Dakota. His beard reached **18.5 FEET** from his chin at the time of his death in 1927. In more modern times, the man with the longest officially confirmed beard is Sarwan Singh, a Canadian music teacher whose beard is 7 feet 7.75 inches long.

NEWS YOU CAN USE

Sleep Is Optional

The longest confirmed stretch that anyone has ever gone without sleep is 276 hours, or 11.5 days. Toimi Soini of Finland managed it in 1964. Supposedly, Maureen Weston of the U.K. surpassed that in 1977 during a rocking-chair marathon that lasted **449 HOURS** (more than 18.5 days), but it's possible that she was able to take micronaps while rocking.

Source: http://www.cbc.ca, http://www.telegraph.co.uk, http://news.bbc.co.uk, http://www.dailymail.co.uk

Luckiest Man in the World

Frano Selak of Croatia has the most amazing luck in the world—both good and bad. He's survived crashes with cars, a bus, a train, and on his only ride ever on a plane. Then in 2005, he won nearly **$1 MILLION** in the Croatian lottery. Five years later, he decided to return to frugality and gave almost all of his money away.

Most Digits...

A Chinese boy was born with 31 digits in total: 15 fingers and 16 toes. In 2010, he had the extra digits removed by surgery and is now down to the more standard 20 digits. Being born with extra digits is a genetic condition called **POLYDACTYLY.**

UNBREAKABLE

Worst Memory

The people with the worst memories are those who suffer from amnesia, which comes in three types. With retrograde amnesia, you can't remember anything from before the moment of the injury that caused the amnesia. With anterograde amnesia, you can't form any new memories. People with **GLOBAL AMNESIA** have both types and can't remember their past or any new memories either!

Best Memory

Brad Williams of La Crosse, Wisconsin, has one of the best **AUTOBIOGRAPHICAL MEMORIES** in the world. Ask him about any date since his early childhood, and he can tell you where he was, what he did, and any historical facts of interest he might have heard about as part of the news at the time. He works as a news anchor for a local radio station.

...Largest Living Baby Ever

The largest baby to be born and survive was the son of Caramina Fidele. Her boy was born in Italy back in 1955 and weighed a stunning **22 POUNDS AND 8 OUNCES** at birth. A larger baby weighing 23 pounds and 12 ounces was born to Anna Bates in Canada back in 1879, but he died less than 12 hours after being born.

Smallest Baby to Survive

With the efforts of research funded by the March of Dimes, more premature babies survive now than ever before. The smallest baby ever born—who survived—is Rumaisa Rahman of Chicago, who weighed only **8.6 OUNCES** when she was born in 2004, 14 weeks early. Her twin sister Hiba weighed 20 ounces, more than twice as much as Rumaisa.

Vegetarian Festival of Pain

During the annual Vegetarian Festival in Phuket, Thailand, many participants **INFLICT TORTURE** on themselves as an offering to the gods. This includes walking on hot coals and shoving multiple large needles through the cheeks of participants, who often bleed little from the puncture wounds, supposedly because of the favor of their gods.

Source: http://www.cbsnews.com, http://www.telegraph.co.uk, http://www.phuket.com

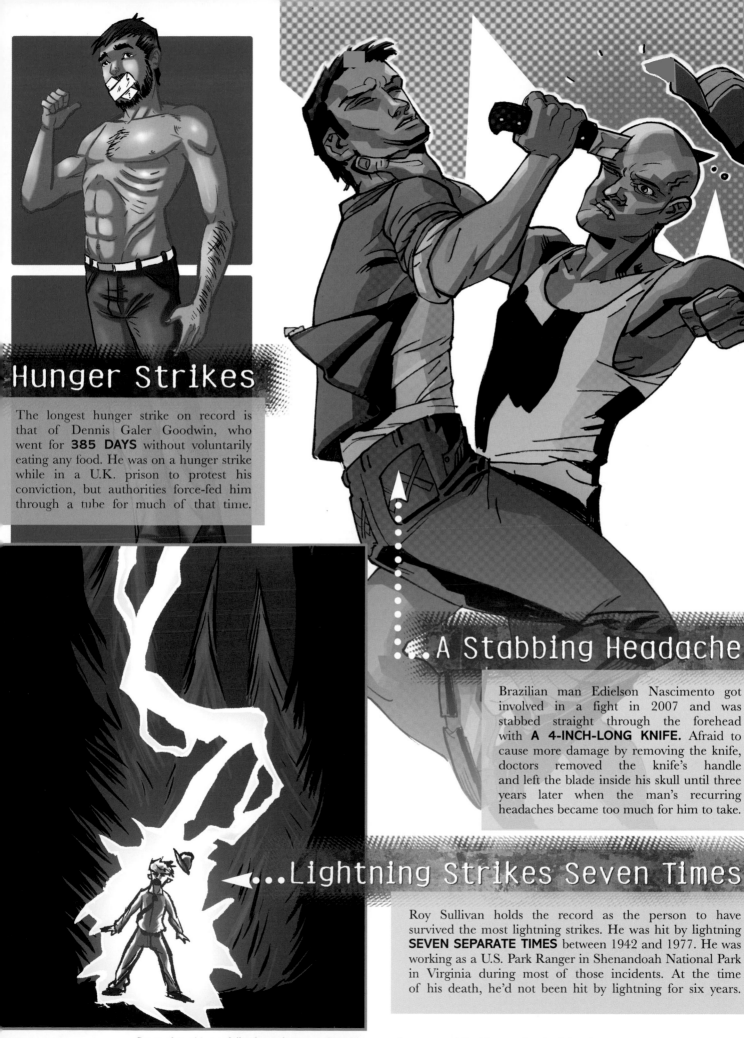

Hunger Strikes

The longest hunger strike on record is that of Dennis Galer Goodwin, who went for **385 DAYS** without voluntarily eating any food. He was on a hunger strike while in a U.K. prison to protest his conviction, but authorities force-fed him through a tube for much of that time.

...A Stabbing Headache

Brazilian man Edielson Nascimento got involved in a fight in 2007 and was stabbed straight through the forehead with **A 4-INCH-LONG KNIFE.** Afraid to cause more damage by removing the knife, doctors removed the knife's handle and left the blade inside his skull until three years later when the man's recurring headaches became too much for him to take.

...Lightning Strikes Seven Times

Roy Sullivan holds the record as the person to have survived the most lightning strikes. He was hit by lightning **SEVEN SEPARATE TIMES** between 1942 and 1977. He was working as a U.S. Park Ranger in Shenandoah National Park in Virginia during most of those incidents. At the time of his death, he'd not been hit by lightning for six years.

Source: http://www.dailytelegraph.com.au, http://www.msnbc.msn.com, http://www.nationalparkstraveler.com

Tongue Record Licked

For years, **ANNIKA IRMLER** of Germany held the record for the world's longest tongue. From the middle of her upper lip to the tip of her tongue measures 2.76 inches. However, in 2006, **STEPHEN TAYLOR** of the U.K. shattered her record with his 3.74-inch-long tongue. It was later measured again and came out even longer at **3.86 INCHES!**

Struck from Space

The first person known to have been **HIT BY A METEORITE** was Ann Hodges of Alabama, who was napping when the 3-pound space rock crashed into her house, bounced off some furniture and bruised her hip. In 2009, another rock struck a teenager in Germany on his hand and then buried itself in the pavement behind him.

The Littlest Sumo

The smallest professional sumo wrestler was Mainoumi Shuhei. Standing only **5 FEET AND 7.5 INCHES,** he was too short to become a sumo wrestler, so he had a doctor inject silicone under his scalp to make him just tall enough. He only weighed 218 pounds, while the largest sumo wrestler was over 600 pounds. Mainoumi beat that wrestler once, but broke his leg doing it.

Source: http://www.space.com, http://halfpie.net, http://www.worldslongesttongue.com/

Lucky at Lotteries

In 2010, Joan Ginther of Texas won more than $1 million for the fourth time by playing the Texas lottery, even though she lives in Las Vegas and only returns to Texas to visit family. She won $5.4 million the first time, $2 million the second, $3 million the third, and $10 million the fourth, for a grand total of **$20.4 MILLION.**

The Echolocator..

BEN UNDERWOOD lost his eyes to cancer but by age 6 trained himself to "see" the world around him by echolocation. He makes a clicking sound with his tongue and can figure out much of his location by how the sound comes back to him, much like a bat or a dolphin. Sadly, cancer took his life in 2009.

···Cut in Half

In 2007, doctors at the Mayo Clinic performed an amazing surgery in which they removed Janis Ollson's bone cancer by **CUTTING HER IN HALF.** They removed one of her legs, the end of her spine, and part of her pelvis. A week later, they put her back together again by fusing her remaining leg to her body with bones taken from the removed leg. Today, she's cancer-free.

NEWS YOU CAN USE
No Kneecaps?

At birth, humans do not have bony kneecaps. At first, they're only made of cartilage, which makes them softer and easier to crawl on. As a kid gets older, **THE CARTILAGE OSSIFIES—** turns into bone. It isn't until a child is between 3 to 5 years old that the kneecap's transformation into bone is complete.

Source: http://www.winnipegfreepress.com, http://abcnews.go.com, http://www.benunderwood.com, http://health.howstuffworks.com

The Unelected President

The only President of the United States to never have been elected to either that position or the Vice Presidency was **GERALD R. FORD**. The Michigan congressman had been appointed to replace Vice President Spiro Agnew in 1973, and then when President Nixon left office in 1974, Ford took over for him, too.

The Lizardman

ERIK SPRAGUE has made a career out of transforming himself into the Lizardman. He's had teeth filed into fangs, his skin tattooed with green scales, Teflon horns implanted above his eyes, and the tip of his tongue split in half to make him seem more lizardlike. A longtime performance artist, he recently recorded his first album with his band Lizard Skynard.

Rumspringa

The Amish live a simple life without many of the trappings (and traps) of modern life. However, when an Amish child turns 16, he or she enters **RUMSPRINGA**. During this time, the teenager is allowed to run wild and experiment with the vices of the modern world until he or she is ready to either be baptized into the church or leave it altogether.

Source: http://www.thelizardman.com, http://www.whitehouse.gov, http://www.npr.org

Face it.......

In 2010, Spanish doctors performed the first **TRANSPLANT OF A FULL FACE.** A young farmer had accidentally shot himself in the face five years before the operation, and he received the skin, lips, teeth, muscles, and cheekbones from a recently deceased donor. He has no scars from his hairline right down to his neck.

The Jumpy Guy

While he was in the Air Force, Don Kellner never once left an airplane in midflight. After he got out, he started parachuting out of perfectly good aircraft on a regular basis. He holds the record for the most parachute jumps, and his current total is **OVER 39,000 JUMPS.**

Most Generous Person

While most of us would like to be rich, not everyone would be willing to give those riches away. **BILL and MELINDA GATES** have donated over **$28 BILLION** to various causes around the world, mostly through the foundation that bears their names. They even inspired fellow billionaire Warren Buffet to pledge $30 billion to their foundation over the next 20 years.

Source: http://www.dkellner.info, http://www.popsci.com, http://news.in.msn.com

GET IN THE ACTION!

Why just read the **BOOK OF EXTREME FACTS** when you can be featured in it yourself? Perhaps this chapter has inspired you to set or share some records of your own, such as:

• Amazing traditions or festivals unique to your culture!
• Odds-defying tales of incredible luck!
• Physical characteristics or skills that stand out in a crowd!

Remember, you are not limited to the above suggestions, or to trying to beat other records in this chapter. Entirely new records are not only allowed… they are encouraged! The only limit is your own creativity. So have some fun (but always remember to keep it SAFE), and if you are younger than 18 remember to ask your parents for permission before attempting any record.

To submit a record:

-Go to *www.bookofextremefacts.com*

-Click on the "Submit New Record" tab

-Provide a brief description of your record and your contact info

-If we decide that your record makes the grade, we will contact you for further details and photos or video of your record

It's just that simple! Good luck…
and **KEEP IT EXTREME!**

Involvement in dangerous sports and related activities carries a significant risk of damage to property, personal injury or death. Please do not endanger yourself or others or take any unnecessary risks. If you choose to participate in dangerous sports or activities in attempting to achieve a distinction that would be recognized in the next edition of Extreme Facts, which IDW does not recommend, you do so at your own risk. IDW suggests the use of professional instruction before entering into any sports or physical activity. You should become knowledgeable about the risks involved. By submitting information to IDW related to inclusion in a future edition of Extreme Facts you assume personal responsibility for your actions and agree to indemnify and hold harmless IDW for the consequences of your actions.

IMAGE CREDITS

Page 114 - MOST TOTAL PIERCINGS Photo by George Gastin
Page 114 - MOST TATTOOS PHOTO by hypersapiens
Page 120 - SMALLEST BABY TO SURVIVE Photo by ceejayoz
Page 120 - VEGETARIAN FESTIVAL OF PAIN Photo by Electrostatico
Page 122 - THE LITTLEST SUMO Photo by FourTildes
Page 122 - THE LITTLEST SUMO Photo by Richard Giles
Page 124 - THE LIZARDMAN Photo by Allen Falkner
Page 124 - RUMSPRINGA Photo by Pasteur
Page 125 - MOST GENEROUS PERSON Photo by Kjetil Ree

CHAPTER 9
BUILDINGS & CONSTRUCTION

Tallest Building in the U.S.

The tallest building in the U.S. is the **WILLIS TOWER** in Chicago, Illinois, which is 1,405 feet and 110 stories tall. When it was finished in 1974, it was the tallest building in the world, and it held that undisputed title until 1998. It was known as the Sears Tower for many years, but Willis Group Holdings—an insurance broker—moved in and bought the naming rights in 2009.

Largest Model of the Solar System

The **ERICSSON GLOBE** in Stockholm, Sweden, serves as a sports and music arena. At over 360 feet across, it's the largest hemispherical building in the world. It's also the Sun in the world's largest model of the Solar System. The Earth sits over 4.5 miles away in the Swedish Museum of Natural History.

The Tallest Building in the World

The title of the tallest building in the world seems to change every few years. In 2011, the undisputed champ is the **BURJ KHALIFA** in Dubai, United Arab Emirates. This 160-story building stands 2,625 feet high—just short of half a mile—shattering all previous records and also making it the tallest structure in the world, period.

Source: http://burjkhalifa.ae, http://willistower.com, http://www.ttt.astro.su.se

The Longest Bridge in the U.S.

The longest bridge in the U.S. is the **LAKE PONTCHARTRAIN CAUSEWAY**, which crosses the wide lake in southern Louisiana. It stretches nearly 24 miles, which makes it the world's longest bridge entirely over water. It's actually two parallel bridges running next to each other on a total of 9,500 pylons.

Deepest Hole

The deepest oil well in history was bored in the Gulf of Mexico by the Deepwater Horizon, which reached a depth of **OVER 35,000 FEET.** That's over 6.5 miles! Sadly, the drilling rig is best known for the disaster that destroyed it in 2010 and caused the worst oil spill ever.

UNBREAKABLE

Brightest Light

The spotlight on the top of the Luxor casino and hotel in Las Vegas is the brightest in the world. Its **43.2 BILLION CANDLEPOWER LIGHT**—which comes from 39 Xenon lamps focused into a single beam—can be seen from outer space and from up to 250 miles away on the Earth.

Oldest Homes in America

The oldest continuously occupied homes in the Unites States are located in the **TAOS PUEBLO** in New Mexico. The first adobe buildings in this town were built between 1,000 and 550 years ago, long before the first European explorers set foot there. About 150 people still call the place home today.

Source: http://engineeringsights.org, http://deepwater.com, http://taospueblo.com, http://luxor.com

CHAPTER 9 • BUILDINGS & CONSTRUCTION

The **WEINAN WEIHE GRAND BRIDGE** is by far the longest bridge in the world. At 49.5 miles, it stretches across the Wei River and many other obstacles in central China. The Zhengzhou-Xi'an High-Speed Railway runs along it. The train's top speed is over 215 miles per hour.

The World's Smallest Nation?

In 1967, Paddy Roy Bates commandeered a World War II-era British defense platform located six miles off the eastern coast of England. Since it was in international waters, he declared it the **PRINCIPALITY OF SEALAND**, an independent nation. While no other country has recognized this claim, Bates and his family have ruled their platform for over 40 years.

SEALAND

Biggest Bookshelf?...

The façade of the garage attached to the Kansas City Public Library in Kansas City, Missouri, along 10th Street, has been made to resemble a **THREE-STORY-TALL** set of books on a community reading shelf. They range from Catch-22 to Romeo and Juliet. Each book is about 25 feet tall and 9 feet wide.

Source: Engineeringsights.org, NationalGeographic.com, http://www.kclibrary.org

Biggest Mall

The world's largest shopping mall (in terms of total area) is the **DUBAI MALL,** which is part of the Burj Khalifa complex. It has over 1,200 shops spread out over more than 12 million square feet—almost half a square mile. It includes a zoo, an aquarium, an ice rink, and the SEGA Republic theme park.

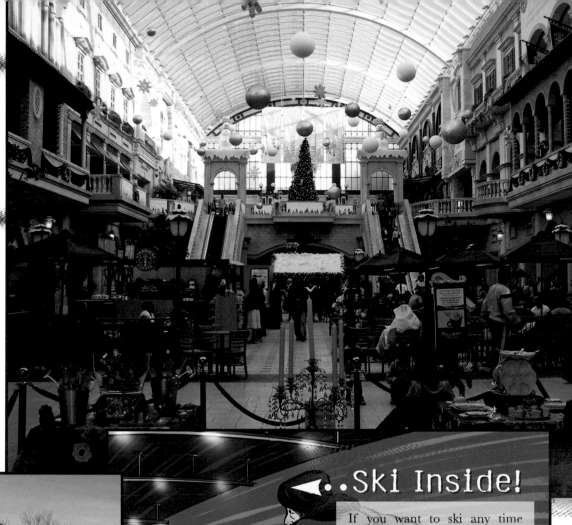

The Beer Can House

In Houston, Texas, John Milkovisch finished paving and decorating his entire lawn to the point at which he had no grass. Then he decided to cover his entire house in **FLATTENED BEER CANS.** He started in 1968 and didn't stop until he finished 18 years later. It's a monument to the power of reusing and recycling.

...Ski Inside!

If you want to ski any time of year, hit an indoor slope and ski on manufactured snow! The first **SNOWWORLD**—was built in the Netherlands in 2001. It's still the largest, with over 8.5 acres of snow. There are dozens of others, ranging from Moscow to Beijing to Dubai, but none in the U.S.—so far.

Spider-Dan!

American daredevil Dan Goodwin made a name for himself by scaling some of the world's tallest structures, including the Willis (then Sears) Tower in Chicago, the Millennium Tower in San Francisco, and the CN Tower in Toronto. He often did so without safety equipment, using only large suction cups, and he dressed in **A HOMEMADE SPIDER-MAN COSTUME!**

Source: http://emaar.com, http://www.beercanhouse.org, http://www.snowworld.com, http://skyscraperman.com

Largest Brick Dome

The building that features the largest masonry dome in the world is the cathedral in Milan known as **THE DUOMO,** or officially as the Basilica di Santa Maria del Fiore (Cathedral of Saint Mary of the Flower). Construction of the Duomo took 142 years and finished in 1436. The dome itself is over 135 feet across.

The Longest Structure

The **GREAT WALL OF CHINA** stretches over 5,500 miles across the nation. Built as a means of keeping out invaders from the north, it took around 2,000 years to complete. A marathon race is run along one length of it every May, but running the whole length would require about 2,100 marathons!

Most Beautiful Tomb

The **TAJ MAHAL** in Agra, India, was built by Emperor Shah Jahan as a memorial to his third wife, Mumtaz Mahal, who gave him 14 children. It took 22 years for 20,000 workers to carve and build the place out of white marble. Its central dome is 58 feet across and stands 213 feet tall.

Source: http://sacred-destinations.com, http://www.islamicity.com, http://www.travelchinaguide.com

The Largest Dam

The largest dam in the world is the **THREE GORGES DAM** in China. It stands over 600 feet tall and stretches 1.3 miles long. The reservoir behind it extends 360 miles upstream, with over 5 trillion gallons of water that swallowed 13 cities, 40 towns, and over a thousand villages, displacing 1.5 million people.

A Large Meal

Beloit, Wisconsin, features the **WORLD'S LARGEST CAN OF CHILI** at its Hormel plant. It's estimated to hold up to 2,000 gallons of the spicy meal. If that's too much to take, you can head up the road to La Crosse, Wisconsin, to find the **WORLD'S LARGEST SIX-PACK OF BEER.**

The Basket Building

When the owner of Longaberger —maker of top-notch baskets of all kinds—wanted to build a home office for his company in Newark, Ohio, he decided to make it look like **THE LARGEST PICNIC BASKET IN THE WORLD**. It stands seven stories tall and comes complete with handles on top!

NEWS YOU CAN USE
Most Visited Spot in the World

The **EIFFEL TOWER** in Paris, France, has long been the most visited spot in the world. Nearly 7 million people per year stop by to see it and get an excellent view of Paris from its decks. That's over 19,000 per day! By the end of 2010, it had hosted over 250 million people.

Source: http://www.pbs.org, http://www.worldslargestthings.com, http://www.longaberger.com, http://www.tour-eiffel.fr

The House on the Rock

West of Madison, Wisconsin, a massive house sits on a **60-FOOT-TALL CHIMNEY OF ROCK.** The owner turned it into a tourist attraction and filled it with odd things and collections, including a three-story bookcase. Its glass-walled Infinity Room has 3,624 windows and stabs 218 feet out from the house. Visitors who walk to the tip can stare straight down at the floor of the forest 156 feet below.

Stay Under the Sea

The first underwater hotel—**JULES' UNDERSEA LODGE**—has been open to the public since 1986. You actually have to scuba dive 21 feet down into the ocean off Key Largo, Florida, to get into the place, and you come up through a hole in the floor and into a pressurized wet room. Each room features a 42-inch round window that lets you watch the sea life swim by.

Cold Lodgings

The first-ever **ICE HOTEL** opened up in Jukkasjärvi, Sweden, back in 1990, hosting its first guests in 1992. The entire place is constructed from ice every year, starting in November, and guests can stay in the place until the end of April, when the place melts into water again. Several other ice hotels are open now, but none are as large as the original.

Source: http://jul.com, http://thehouseontherock.com, http://icehotel.com

The Rotating Skyscraper....

Architect David Fisher has designed a **ROTATING SKYSCRAPER** and has plans to build one in Dubai. It will be 80 stories tall, and each floor will be able to rotate independently on a central axis. Each story will also have its own wind turbine, making the building entirely self-powered.

Biggest Flower Building

The Bahá'í House of Worship in New Delhi, India—also known as the **LOTUS TEMPLE**—is a gigantic temple designed to look like a 9-sided flower with 27 petals. It is open to people of all faiths, and it quickly became the most popular destination in India, surpassing even the Taj Mahal.

The Sculptured House

High in the foothills of the Rocky Mountains, overlooking I-70 to the west of Denver, sits the **SCULPTURED HOUSE.** Meant to be built entirely of curves, there are only two right angles in the entire place. Woody Allen used it as a house of the future in his movie *Sleeper*, but the place sat unfinished for over 30 years until it was purchased in 1999.

UNBREAKABLE

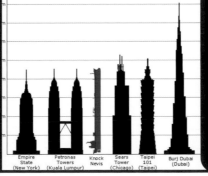

Empire State (New York)	Petronas Towers (Kuala Lumpur)	Knock Nevis	Sears Tower (Chicago)	Taipei 101 (Taipei)	Burj Dubai (Dubai)

World's Largest Ship

The **KNOCK NEVIS** is the largest ship ever built. At 1,500 feet long, if you could stand her on end she would reach taller than the top floor of the Willis Tower in Chicago. She is too large to maneuver through the English Channel. In 2010, she was permanently docked in India to be scrapped.

Source: http://www.bahaindia.org, http://www.architectureforsale.com, http://news.bbc.co.uk, http://www.maritime-connector.com

NEWS YOU CAN USE

Longest Trafficked Tunnel

In 2010, the Swiss broke through the longest train tunnel in the world, which measures 35.4 miles. Once the tracks laid through it open up in 2017, you'll be able to **BUZZ BENEATH THE ALPS ON A BULLET TRAIN.** At its top speed of 155 miles per hour, you'll only be under the mountain for less than 14 minutes!

The Longest Tunnel

The longest tunnel in the world is the 85-mile Delaware Aqueduct, which carries about half of New York City's drinking water to it from the Catskill Mountains. That's about **500 MILLION GALLONS A DAY,** in addition to the 35 million or so gallons the aqueduct loses to leaks every day. Repairs to the leaks should be completed in 2019.

Largest Football Stadium

The largest football stadium in the world is **MICHIGAN STADIUM** in Ann Arbor, Michigan, home of the University of Michigan Wolverines. Known as the Big House, it officially seats 109,901, but it regularly breaks that number by a couple thousand extra fans. Most of the stadium sits below ground, leaving only the upper 20 rows or so above the earth.

Source: http://towercrane.com, http://www.msnbc.msn.com, http://www.umich.edu

..The Largest Monster

Ancient Egypt loved the sphinx, a lion with a woman's head and a bird's wings. The **GREAT SPHINX** of Giza, Egypt, is the largest such creature around at 240 feet long and 66 feet high. It was built around 4,500 years ago, and it was once painted with bright colors that have since worn away.

UNBEATABLE

Look Straight Down

The **GRAND CANYON SKYWALK** is a glass-bottomed pedestrian bridge that circles 70 feet out over the edge of the Grand Canyon. Standing on it, you can safely peer down at the canyon floor 4,000 feet below. That's about as tall as the Willis Tower—if you stacked it on top of the Burj Khalifa.

Largest Sporting Facility

The **INDIANAPOLIS MOTOR SPEEDWAY** is the largest sports facility in the world. It can seat more than 250,000 people around its track, and it covers 1,025 acres, more than 1.5 square miles. The track itself runs 2.5 miles, which means a racer must circle it 200 times to finish the famed Indianapolis 500.

..The Tallest Statue

The **SPRING TEMPLE BUDDHA,** in China, stands 420 feet tall, including a 66-foot base, making it the tallest statue in the world. If you count the pedestal below, it comes to over 680 feet tall. Made of over 1,100 pieces of cast copper, it weighs over 1,100 tons. It shows the Budda standing with one hand raised and the other stretched low.

Source: http://www.indianapolismotorspeedway.com, http://touregypt.net, http://www.worldsbiggests.com, http://www.grandcanyonskywalk.com

...Hot Stuff

The world's **LARGEST SOLAR FURNACE** is located in Font-Romeu-Odeillo-Via, France. It is nine stories tall, and its 10,000 mirrors collect enough sunlight to bring the temperature at its focal spot up to 5,430° F. It is used to melt metals. Don't try to toast your bagel with it!

Highest Bungee Jump

The highest commercial bungee jump ever operated ran from the U.S.' highest suspension bridge: the Royal Gorge Bridge in Colorado, which hangs more than 1,050 feet above the Arkansas River. At that height, **YOU CAN HIT TERMINAL VELOCITY** before the cord starts to pull. It was only allowed during the annual Go Fast Games, though, which started in 2003 and ended in 2008.

Dr. Seuss' Library

The **GEISEL LIBRARY** at the University of California-San Diego was named for Theodor Geisel (Dr. Seuss) and his wife Audrey. Its lower two stories are a pedestal upon which the upper six stories, which form a stepped tower, rest. It looks like something that could have sprung from the stories of Dr. Seuss!

Source: http://atlasobscura.com, http://www.loc.gov, http://libraries.ucsd.edu

Longest Road

The longest road in the world is the **PAN-AMERICAN HIGHWAY,** which reaches from Prudhoe Bay, Alaska, all the way to Ushuaia, Argentina. That's about 16,000 miles. There's a short gap of 54 miles on the border between Panama and Columbia. Plans are underway to take on this last hurdle soon, but concerns for the rainforest through which it would pass have stalled it.

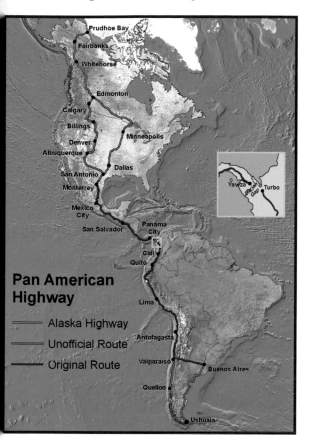

Prudhoe Bay
Fairbanks
Whitehorse
Edmonton
Calgary
Billings
Denver
Albuquerque
Minneapolis
San Antonio
Dallas
Monterrey
Mexico City
San Salvador
Panama City
Cali
Quito
Lima
Antofagasta
Valparaiso
Buenos Aires
Quellon
Ushuaia
Yaviza Darién Gap Turbo

Pan American Highway

— Alaska Highway
— Unofficial Route
— Original Route

The Blur Building

The **BLUR BUILDING** in Switzerland was constructed atop a set of 31,500 fog nozzles. These form a fog bank around the building's base that makes it seem as if it is floating in midair above a cloud. To reach the building, you have to walk down a 400-foot ramp that becomes enveloped by the fog. It features a water bar with drinks of H2O from places around the world.

Largest Office Building

The largest office building in the world—in terms of floor space—is the **PENTAGON**, the home of the United States Department of Defense. About 23,000 people work there among its 17.5 miles of corridors. Despite this, because of its design, it should only take about seven minutes to walk from any one place in the building to another.

NEWS YOU CAN USE

Largest Passenger Ship

The largest passenger ship in the world is the Royal Caribbean cruise ship **OASIS OF THE SEAS**. It stretches nearly 1,200 feet long, has 16 decks, and can carry up to 5,400 paying passengers at a time. It has seven different neighborhoods on board, including a sports zone that occupies an entire deck and features four pools and a water park.

Source: http://wired.com, http://pentagon.afis.osd.mil, http://www.cnn.com, http://www.royalcaribbean.com

GET IN THE ACTION!

Why just read the **BOOK OF EXTREME FACTS** when you can be featured in it yourself? Perhaps this chapter has inspired you to set or share some records of your own, such as:

• Wild and wacky buildings of all shapes and sizes!
• Roadside attractions like giant shoe houses or mammoth monuments!
• Eco-friendly homes and offices that show us a glimpse of the future!

Remember, you are not limited to the above suggestions, or to trying to beat other records in this chapter. Entirely new records are not only allowed… they are encouraged! The only limit is your own creativity. So have some fun (but always remember to keep it SAFE), and if you are younger than 18 remember to ask your parents for permission before attempting any record.

To submit a record:

-Go to *www.bookofextremefacts.com*

-Click on the "Submit New Record" tab

-Provide a brief description of your record and your contact info

-If we decide that your record makes the grade, we will contact you for further details and photos or video of your record

It's just that simple! Good luck…
and **KEEP IT EXTREME!**

Involvement in dangerous sports and related activities carries a significant risk of damage to property, personal injury or death. Please do not endanger yourself or others or take any unnecessary risks. If you choose to participate in dangerous sports or activities in attempting to achieve a distinction that would be recognized in the next edition of Extreme Facts, which IDW does not recommend, you do so at your own risk. IDW suggests the use of professional instruction before entering into any sports or physical activity. You should become knowledgeable about the risks involved. By submitting information to IDW related to inclusion in a future edition of Extreme Facts you assume personal responsibility for your actions and agree to indemnify and hold harmless IDW for the consequences of your actions.

IMAGE CREDITS

Page 128 - THE TALLEST BUILDING in the World Photo by
        Titoni Thomas
Page 128 - TALLEST BUILDING IN THE U.S. Photo by Daniel Schwen
Page 129 - BRIGHTEST LIGHT Photo by Stephen Witherden
Page 130 - THE LONGEST BRIDGE IN THE WORLD Photo by
        ASDFGH at en.wikipedia
Page 131 - THE BEER CAN HOUSE Photo by NZ Russ
Page 131 - SPIDER-DAN Photo by Mimiken
Page 131 - SPIDER-DAN Photo by Rusewcrazy
Page 132 - LARGEST BRICK DOME Photo by MarcusObal
Page 132 - THE LONGEST STRUCTURE Photo by Samxli
Page 132 - MOST BEAUTIFUL TOMB Photo by Yann
Page 133 - THE LARGEST DAM Photo by Rehman
Page 134 - THE HOUSE ON THE ROCK Photo by Richie Diesterheft
Page 135 - BIGGEST FLOWER BUILDING Photo by Mark Pellegrini
Page 135 - THE SCULPTURED HOUSE Photo by Elizabeth
Page 135 - WORLD'S LARGEST SHIP Photo by Delphine Ménard
Page 136 - THE LONGEST TUNNEL Photo by Derek Ramsey
Page 137 - LOOK STRAIGHT DOWN Photo by Jonas.tesch
Page 137 - LARGEST SPORTING FACILITY Photo by Rick Dikeman
Page 138 - HIGHEST BUNGEE JUMP Photo by Larry D. Moore
Page 138 - DR. SEUSS' LIBRARY Photo by belisario
Page 139 - LONGEST ROAD Photo by Seaweege
Page 139 - THE BLUR BUILDING Photo by Norbert Aepli
Page 139 - LARGEST PASSENGER SHIP Photo by Baldwin040

CHAPTER 10
THE ANCIENT WORLD

NEWS YOU CAN USE

Key to the Ancient World

This chapter delves deep into the past. To help keep things straight, the titles of the items in this section are color-coded to let you know just when the event is taking place. In the case of events that stretch over two periods, the item is coded to the period in which it began.

ORANGE–prehistory to 3000 BC
BLUE–1800 BC to 1000 BC
RED–900 BC to 27 BC
PURPLE–75 AD to 1300 AD
BLACK–multiple eras

New Dinosaur Discoveries

Before humankind, Earth was ruled by the dinosaurs, and we learn more about these ancient creatures every day. Two rhino-sized species related to the Triceratops were recently identified in Utah. One, the **KOSMOCERATOPS**, sported 15 horns in a frill designed to attract mates. Meanwhile, the **BRACHYLOPHOSAURUS**, discovered in Montana, had a head topped with a large bony plate shaped like a modern bike helmet—perhaps used for ramming.

Oldest Humans

The recipient of the title of oldest human depends on how you define "human." For many scientists, it is the ability to stand upright, and **HOMINIDAE** did that six to seven million years ago. If you are talking about **HOMO SAPIENS,** or modern humans, then the earliest known people lived about 150,000 years ago in the land we now know as Ethiopia.

Source: http://news.yahoo.com, http://www.amnh.org

Earliest Art

While art in the form of carvings and pounded indentations in rock date to the very beginnings of humankind, the earliest art in the form of "drawing" is represented in the cave paintings of France. These paintings show animals of the period, such as bison, horses, and the deer-like cervid. The earliest examples are found in the **GROTTE CHAUVET** cave and were painted between 32,000 and 30,000 years ago during the Upper Paleolithic Period.

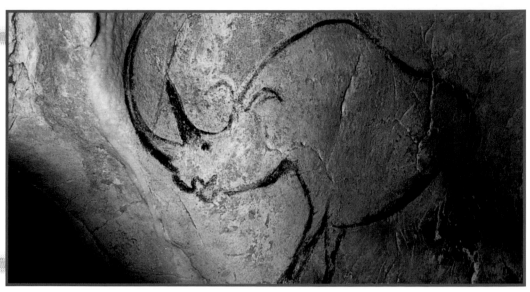

Birth Of Metallurgy

The discovery that lifted humankind out of the Stone Age was the birth of **METALLURGY**, or the ability to make metal. Probably an accidental discovery arising out of copper separating from pottery materials when the clay was baked, the methods of metal extraction—called smelting—were refined over the centuries. Metallurgy was discovered at different times in different places around the globe, but the earliest successes seemed to have occurred in the Balkans and western Asia between 7000 and 6000 BC.

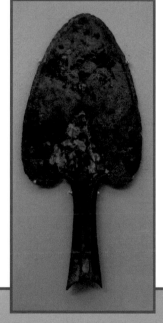

NEWS YOU CAN USE

Papyrus Making

The invention of paper-like papyrus was a revolutionary development in ancient Egypt, and now you can make some, too!

1) Harvest mature papyrus plants and remove the inner, non-green part called the pith.

2) Cut the pith into long strips, beat them flat, and steep in water for 3 days until soft.

3) Lay overlapping strips horizontally on an absorbent cotton pad, then lay more strips vertically on top.

4) Cover with another cotton pad and press repeatedly until dry. Now grab that quill and write some hieroglyphics!

Mummies!

The art of mummification—the preservation of a body after death—is most famous in Egypt but has occurred all over the world. The first mummies were created by chance, when physical geography like dry sands or peat bogs acted as the preserving agents, but the Egyptians elevated the practice to a high art. Before being wrapped, the brain was removed through the nose using long hooks and was discarded. The internal organs were stored in containers called **CANOPIC JARS,** with specifically decorated lids: falcon for the intestines, jackal for the stomach, baboon for the lungs, and a human head for the liver.

The Phoenicians

The Phoenicians were the greatest seafarers of the ancient world, which allowed them to spread their civilization and ideas far beyond their homeland. Their name was given to them by the Greeks and means "Purple Men," perhaps referring to the dyed cloth they traded, although they called themselves the "Kinahu," or Canaanites. Their most lasting legacy to the modern world is their **ALPHABET:** almost ALL of the alphabets people use today were derived from the Phoenicians.

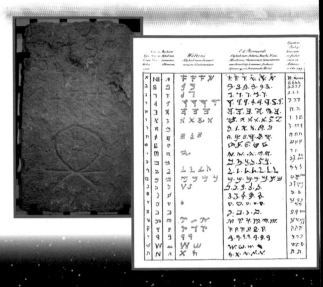

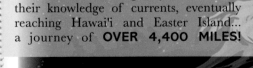

Pacific Crossings...▶

Although a truly ancient migration out of South China around 30,000 years ago helped populate Indonesia and Papua New Guinea, the islands of the South Pacific remained uninhabited. Then a second wave of migration filled the islands with their current Melanesian and Polynesian populations. These seafarers crossed vast swaths of ocean using only the stars and their knowledge of currents, eventually reaching Hawai'i and Easter Island... a journey of **OVER 4,400 MILES!**

Source: http://www.si.umich.edu, http://www.lost-civilizations.net, http://www.pacific-travel-guides.com

Located just below the kingdoms of ancient Egypt, Kush was a flourishing trade site. It was conquered by its northern neighbors but managed to regain freedom around 750 BC. Kush still retained a strong Egyptian influence, however, which is evident even in late-period buildings like the temple dedicated to the lion god Apemedek. Scaffolding was built on the cliffs above the capital of Napata and used to reach otherwise inaccessible rock faces, where the Kushites carved hieroglyphics in honor of their kings, that were then covered in **SHEETS OF PURE GOLD.** A Kushite language slowly developed to replace heiroglyphics, but it has yet to be deciphered.

Babylon

Although the origins of Babylon may stretch beyond recorded history, what is known displays the remarkable survivability of the city. It first gained fame as the capital of Hammurabi, who devised and enforced one of the world's first law codes. For the next 1,100 years, Babylon was repeatedly conquered by waves of invaders... except the invaders always chose to give up their own customs in favor of the Babylonians'! It reached a second period of greatness under Nebuchadnezzar II, boasting giant city walls, the famed hanging gardens of Babylon, and the Esagila, a **GIANT ZIGGURAT-SHAPED TEMPLE** dedicated to Marduk, the city's god.

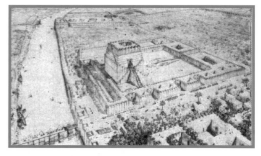

The Valley Of The Kings

The Valley of the Kings in Egypt holds the splendor of ancient Egypt beneath its sands. The valley, used for the tombs of royals and nobles for over four and a half centuries, contains over **60 KNOWN BURIAL SITES.** The tombs, which took about 6 years each to build, were designed to foil grave robbers—but to no avail, as almost all were ransacked to some degree. The tomb of Amenhotep contained the mummies of four pharoahs and nine others, while Tuthmose III's burial room could only be reached by climbing stairs and then crossing a deep pit built as a trap for the unsuspecting. The most famous pharoah of all, Tutankhamun, was also buried here, lying undetected until the astounding collection of ancient treasure that accompanied him in death was discovered in 1922.

Stonehenge

Stonehenge, in southern England, still retains many mysteries. For example, it is clear that Stonehenge was a sacred site, and is used even today for these purposes by modern-day Druids and pagans. However, the actual religion of its first builders is unknown to us. Stonehenge began as a simple circular ditch, but was expanded to a series of two concentric circles of upright stones, with the outer ring topped by cross-stones. Inside the circle was a horseshoe pattern that aligned perfectly with the midsummer sunrise. Perhaps most mysteriously, many of the nearly 4-ton stones were not quarried locally, but instead were cut and transported from a site **ALMOST 250 MILES AWAY.**

Mound-Building People

North America was home to three distinct mound-building civilizations. The earliest were the Adena, who built the Serpent Mound, which measured 4 to 5 feet high and stretched for 1,330 feet. Next came the Hopewell civilization, which was followed by the Mississippians, the greatest builders of them all. **MONK'S MOUND**, home of their chief, covered a full 16 acres and stood 110 feet high. It was created one bucket at a time and took 300 years to build.

Scythians!

Believed to have originated in what is now Iran, the Scythians were a fierce nomadic people that spread throughout the ancient world, thanks to their expert horsemanship. They were also accomplished archers, using a special double-curved bow. Like modern-day motorcycle gangs, the Scythians' bodies—men and women alike—were almost fully covered in intricate tribal tattoos. The women fought alongside the men in battle, and Greek historian Herodotus reported that they used the **SKULLS OF THEIR DEFEATED ENEMIES** as drinking cups!

Source: http://www.sacred-destinations.com, http://www.watertown.k12.ma.us, http://www.lost-civilizations.net

UNBREAKABLE

The Largest Stone Buddha

Sitting calmly above the confluence of three Chinese rivers, the **LESHAN GIANT BUDDHA** is the largest carved stone Buddha in the world. The statue, which took over 90 years to complete, is 233 feet from top to bottom. The shoulders are 92 feet wide—enough room for a basketball court! The monk Hai Tong was the force behind the statue, begging for 20 years to raise sufficient funds for its construction. When local officials tried to get their hands on the money, Hai Tong said they could have his eye instead, and promptly gouged it out while the horrified officials retreated.

Petra

Ancient capital of the Nabataeans, Petra is a **HIDDEN CITY CARVED FROM SOLID ROCK** in Wadi Musa, Jordan. It can be reached only by going through a 1,000-yard-long gorge with 260-foot-high cliffs known as the Siq. The Siq leads directly to al-Khazneh, or the Treasury, a massive tomb gouged from the red cliffs that stands almost 100 feet wide and 150 feet high. The city is packed with features such as a "street" of Nabataean cliff tombs, a 4,000-seat theater, and the immense Great Temple. Another giant site, the Ad-Deir Monastery, sits farther up in the valley, and takes a climb up 800 rock-hewn steps to reach.

Cyrus & Darius

Cyrus of Persia, devoted to his religion of Zoroastrianism, was determined to spread it far and wide, and embarked on a campaign of conquest. Cyrus was the first leader in history who had the idea to **CONQUER THE ENTIRE WORLD**. Upon his death, his empire stretched from the coasts of Turkey down through Syria and Israel, across Iraq and Iran and up to the Aral Sea. His grandson, Darius, pushed even farther, bringing the battle to the gates of Athens before finally being repulsed at the Battle of Marathon. Had the Persians won, Greek civilization as we know it would likely have never come into being.

Source: http://www.travelchinaguide.com, http://www.visitjordan.com, http://www.wsu.edu

Greek Democracy

Greece has long been acknowledged as the birthplace of western civilization. It was here that Cleisthenes of Athens introduced democracy to his city. The word "democracy" itself means **"PEOPLE POWER"** in Greek. Philosophers like Socrates and Aristotle and mathematicians such as Pythagoras and Euclid all called Athens home. Democracy lasted in its Athenian birthplace for 186 years, until Philip of Macedon, father of Alexander the Great, conquered the city.

...Axum

Axum was the name shared by both a city and a kingdom in what is now Ethiopia. From here, the Queen of Sheba ruled. The son of the Queen and Israel's King David, Meniopk, became Ethiopia's first emperor, and is said to have brought the Ark of the Covenant back to the country. The Ark is said to contain the tablets on which the Ten Commandments are written, and Ethiopians believe they **STILL RESIDE IN THE CHURCH OF ST. MARY OF ZION** there. Today, all that remains of the ancient city are a series of huge granite pillars, some as high as 20 to 30 meters.

Alexander The Great

Alexander the Great, tutored by the Greek philosopher Aristotle, started his illustrious career at 16, crushing an uprising in Macedonia while his father the king was away with his army. As king himself, Alexander began the military campaigning that would make him **HISTORY'S GREATEST CONQUEROR.** He pushed east into Asia Minor, eventually conquering the mighty Egyptians and Persians. But Alexander was not satisfied, and he pushed his army into India before they had enough and refused to go farther. He died in Babylon on his way back to Macedonia, and the greatest empire the world had ever seen was soon broken up.

Source: http://travel.newarchaeology.com, http://www.selamta.net, http://faq.macedonia.org

The Terra Cotta Army

The discovery of Qin Shi Huang's terra cotta army electrified the world in 1974. Begun as a tomb complex as soon as the emperor gained power at age 13, it took a full 11 years and 700,000 workers to complete. The three pits discovered so far house a series of around **8,000 LIFE-SIZED SOLDIER STATUES, PLUS CHARIOTS, HORSES, AND EVEN WEAPONS.** Still, what remains undiscovered may be the most amazing of all. According to a report written 100 years after the site was built, the central chamber is piled high with treasure, has a pearl-studded roof to represent the starry sky, and has a floor forming a stone map of the Chinese kingdom complete with rivers of mercury.

The Lighthouse At Alexandria ...

Alexandria was an Egyptian port that received ships from both the Nile River and the Mediterranean Sea. Here the first lighthouse was constructed in 270 BC. When it was completed, it was second in height to only the Great Pyramid, **RISING TO AROUND 450 FEET.** Fires were burned at the top and a burnished mirror used to make it visible up to 100 miles away. When Sostrates, its designer, was denied permission to carve his own name on the structure, he did anyway... but hid it under a layer of plaster bearing the name of his ruler. But in time, the plaster chipped away and Sostrates cleverly got his wish.

Masada

Masada, a fortress constructed on a rocky outcropping between the Dead Sea and the Judean desert, was first constructed by King Herod to protect himself from perceived threats from the Jewish people. Its next occupiers after Herod, the Romans, were in fact displaced by a Jewish rebel group known as the Zealots. It remained in Jewish hands after Rome took Jerusalem in 70 AD, with defeated fighters making their way there to stage a last-gasp resistance effort. A long **TWO-YEAR SIEGE** began, with a ramp built by Jewish slaves up to the top of the rock, finally allowing a Roman battering ram access to the fortress walls. Once they were breached, however, a second wall was hastily erected. The small force inside, however, knew that defeat was near at hand, and decided to commit mass suicide rather than submit to defeat at the hands of the Romans. This symbol of Jewish resistance is still revered today—Israeli soldiers take an oath upon joining the military that Masada shall not fall again.

Source: http://opa.yale.edu, http://map.gsfc.nasa.gov, http://www.planetary.org, http://quest.nasa.gov

Roman Engineering

The Roman Empire is responsible for countless achievements in art, science, and warfare. Perhaps their most lasting contributions to history, however, were their astonishing achievements in engineering. Structures such as the Coliseum, the 93-foot-high aqueduct in Segovia, Spain, and countless amphitheaters still stand today. The Romans also invented and improved on many things that made daily life more enjoyable, such as well-maintained roads, heated bath complexes, **PUBLIC BATHROOMS** and sewage systems, running water in homes, and a central air system for keeping buildings warm.

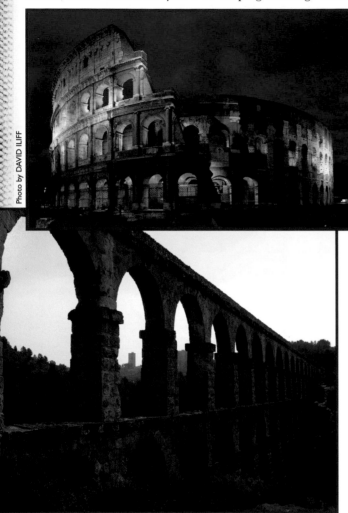

Photo by DAVID ILIFF

Greek Vending Machine

Vending machines dispense all sorts of things and seem like modern marvels, but the truth is they aren't modern at all. In fact, the Greek inventor Heron made one **ALMOST 2,000 YEARS AGO!** His invention dispensed holy water to worshipers entering a temple. A coin was dropped into a slot and came to rest on a metal pan, where its weight pushed the pan down to open a valve and dispense water. Once the coin's weight made the pan tilt at a severe angle, the coin would slide off and return the pan to an upright position, shutting the valve off. Heron invented all sorts of other things as well, including the world's first steam engine, a self-feeding water fountain, and a force pump used in the ancient world as a fire engine.

Hadrian's Wall

When Hadrian became leader of Rome, its empire stretched all the way to present-day Great Britain. The Roman settlers there, however, suffered constant attacks and harassment from the Picts, who lived in what we call Scotland today. As protection, Hadrian ordered the building of a wall that would mark the northern border of Rome's territory and whose defensive capabilities were formidable indeed. Hadrian's Wall was 15 feet high and 10 feet wide and stretched all the way from the Irish Sea to the North Sea. Its entire 73-mile (or 80 Roman mile) length was **STUDDED WITH FORTIFICATIONS:** 16 forts holding up to 1,000 soldiers were placed along it, while every Roman mile there were smaller forts of 60 soldiers. A watchtower was placed every third of a mile, and in the event the wall was breached, a ditch was placed immediately to its south to further discourage invaders.

Source: http://www.historylearningsite.co.uk, http://www.smith.edu, http://ancienthistory.about.com

Temple Of Gold & Diamonds

The **SHWEDAGON PAGODA** in Yangon, Myanmar, is the country's holiest Buddhist shrine. Said to contain several hairs of the Buddha himself, it was rescued from a semi-ruined and jungle-overgrown state by Indian emperor Asoka in antiquity. The stupa, or main dome, is covered top to bottom with gold leaf, gold plates, and silver. Embedded in the gold are precious stones, including 5,451 diamonds, and it is topped by a single massive 76-carat diamond.

Teotihuacan

The great city of Teotihuacan in Mexico once was home to almost 200,000 people, but it declined and disappeared as mysteriously as it arose. All that remains are the impressive monuments of the city center. The **PYRAMID OF THE SUN** is the third-largest pyramid in the world at 250 feet high and 650 feet square. **THE CIUDADELA** is an enormous plaza capable of holding 100,000 people and also contains the Feathered Serpent pyramid, which was probably a ritual center. **THE PYRAMID OF THE MOON** lies at the north end of the city. Its position, as well as the position of the entire city's grid, is laid out with mathematical precision that shows the culture that built it had advanced knowledge of astronomy. However, there is much we still don't know about Teotihuacan.

Great Zimbabwe

Built on an elevated plain to escape the sleeping sickness spread by tsetse flies in low-lying areas, Great Zimbabwe was once home to around 18,000 people. The hill complex contained the areas for smelting metals, but more importantly it was the site of the ritual enclosure used by the king and the treasuries where his treasure was stored. The valley complex, where the king and the majority of the population lived, contains the most impressive of the city's features, the **IMBA HURU,** or Great Enclosure. Constructed from about 900,000 granite fragments fitted together without mortar of any kind, it rose 32 feet from the valley floor and stretched for 800 feet.

Source: http://www.sacred-destinations.com, http://www.world-mysteries.com, http://www.manuampim.com

Montezuma's Castle

Lying just south of Sedona, Arizona, Montezuma's Castle is a remarkable dwelling place set in a steep cliff far above the valley below. Its present name is a mistake, given to it by explorers who thought they'd found an example of Aztec architecture. In fact, the site was abandoned by the Sinaqua tribe, its actual builders, over 100 years before the Aztec Montezuma was even born! It's also not a castle at all, but rather a sort of five-story apartment building containing 20 separate rooms. It was **ALMOST IMPOSSIBLE TO ATTACK,** since it was reached by using a series of ladders which were then pulled up to prevent invaders from accessing it.

Early Musical .....Instruments

The urge to create and listen to music stretches back to our proto-human ancestors. The very first instrument was the human voice, followed by simple percussion using rocks. The **OLDEST CREATED INSTRUMENT** yet found was a four-note bone flute used by Neanderthals 67,000 years ago. Drums came next, with the oldest example appearing 30,000 years after the bone flute. Stringed lyres were present in ancient Sumeria around 2500 BC, and a fragment of a cuneiform tablet from that time represents the first example of musical notation. Around the same time, in Southeast Asia, the xylophone was invented. Also around that date, an early horn called the lurer was used in Scandinavia, capable of producing 12 to 14 notes.

Source: http://www.dreamsedona.com, http://www.smashinglists.com

Ancient Weapons Of War

War is as old as humanity itself, and humans throughout the ages have created weaponry designed to cause maximum death and destruction.

GREEK FIRE was an early flamethrower, with a still-unknown substance heated on the deck of a ship and shot from a large deck-mounted syringe to rain down on enemies.

CALTROPS were shaped like jacks and made of sharpened spikes, all the better to penetrate the soft feet of camels and war elephants, or the hooves of cavalry horses.

ARBALESTS were giant crossbows, whose size made them able to fire very deadly bolts with high accuracy up to about 1,600 feet. In fact, they were so deadly that they were banned in 1139 by the Pope for warfare against other Christians.

The **TREBUCHET** was a high-powered catapult used to besiege a walled or fortified city by hurling projectiles at it, or diseased corpses and beehives over the walls.

Another unique weapon used in siege warfare were **DEAD BODIES,** which were placed in the the fresh water supply leading to the walled city being attacked until its inhabitants took sick with plague and were easy pickings.

The protectors of walled cities were not without their own defenses, however. The walls were often studded with openings called **MURDER HOLES** through which rocks or arrows could be fired. Their most horrific use, though, occured when boiling oil or water was poured through them, drenching attackers with a killing flood of burning death.

GET IN THE ACTION!

Why just read the **BOOK OF EXTREME FACTS** when you can be featured in it yourself? Perhaps this chapter has inspired you to set or share some records of your own, such as:

• Ancient earthworks like forts or Native American dwellings near you!
• Fascinating finds, such as arrowheads or dinosaur bones!
• Great cultures of the past that more people need to know about!

Remember, you are not limited to the above suggestions, or to trying to beat other records in this chapter. Entirely new records are not only allowed… they are encouraged! The only limit is your own creativity. So have some fun (but always remember to keep it SAFE), and if you are younger than 18 remember to ask your parents for permission before attempting any record.

To submit a record:

-Go to *www.bookofextremefacts.com*

-Click on the "Submit New Record" tab

-Provide a brief description of your record and your contact info

-If we decide that your record makes the grade, we will contact you for further details and photos or video of your record

It's just that simple! Good luck…
and **KEEP IT EXTREME!**

Involvement in dangerous sports and related activities carries a significant risk of damage to property, personal injury or death. Please do not endanger yourself or others or take any unnecessary risks. If you choose to participate in dangerous sports or activities in attempting to achieve a distinction that would be recognized in the next edition of Extreme Facts, which IDW does not recommend, you do so at your own risk. IDW suggests the use of professional instruction before entering into any sports or physical activity. You should become knowledgeable about the risks involved. By submitting information to IDW related to inclusion in a future edition of Extreme Facts you assume personal responsibility for your actions and agree to indemnify and hold harmless IDW for the consequences of your actions.

IMAGE CREDITS

Page 143 - THE BIRTH OF METALLURGY
          Photo by Classical Numismatic Group, Inc.
Page 143 - THE BIRTH OF METALLURGY
          Photo by Eduard von der Heydt and Dr. Rudolph Schmidt
Page 143 - METALLURGY Photo by PHGCOM
Page 144 - THE PHOENICIANS Photo by Golf Bravo
Page 145 - THE VALLEY OF THE KINGS Photo by Nikola Smolenski
Page 146 - STONEHENGE Photo by David Bjorgen
Page 146 - MOUND-BUILDING PEOPLE Photo by Skubasteve834
Page 147 - THE LARGEST STONE BUDDHA Photo by Bernt Rostad
Page 147 - PETRA Photo by David Bjorgen
Page 148 - GREEK DEMOCRACY Photo by www.ohiochannel.org
Page 148 - ALEXANDER THE GREAT Photo by Magrippa
Page 148 - ALEXANDER THE GREAT Photo by Yair Haklai
Page 149 - THE TERRA COTTA ARMY Photo by Maros
Page 150 - ROMAN ENGINEERING Photo by DAVID ILIFF
          http://creativecommons.org/licenses/by-sa/2.5/deed.en
Page 150 - ROMAN ENGINEERING Photo by Pamela McCreight
Page 150 - HADRIAN'S WALL Photo by Glen Bowman
Page 151 - TEMPLE OF GOLD & DIAMONDS Photo by Colegota
Page 151 - TEMPLE OF GOLD & DIAMONDS Photo by
          Government of Thailand
Page 151 - TEOTIHUACAN Photo by Peter Andersen
Page 153 - CALTROPS Photo by Badseed
Page 153 - ARBALESTS Photo by Rama
Page 153 - TREBUCHET Photo by Thesupermat
Page 153 - DEAD BODIES Photo by Damnonii
Page 153 - MURDER HOLES Photo by Canadacow

CHAPTER 11
GAMES & ENTERTAINMENT

... First War Game

The first published war game was *Little Wars*, designed and written by **H. G. Wells**, author of *The Time Machine*, *The War of the Worlds*, and many other early science fiction novels. It simulated military battles with miniatures, and it also featured the first gaming-related fiction ever written.

First Video Game

The first video game was created in 1947 by Thomas T. Goldsmith Jr. and Settle Ray Mann. It was a missile simulator called the **CATHODE RAY TUBE AMUSEMENT DEVICE,** and players used analog controls to aim a dot on the screen. Since it didn't use a computer, there were no graphics. Instead, the game used clear overlays placed on the screen.

Most Popular Game Series

The bestselling video game series of all time is Nintendo's line of Mario games, which have sold over 220 million copies. Another Nintendo line—*Pokémon*—comes in a close second with more than 200 million copies sold. However, the board game **MONOPOLY** has sold over 250 million copies, beating them both.

NEWS YOU CAN USE

The Museum of Play

The Strong Museum of Play in Rochester, New York, is a Smithsonian-affiliated museum dedicated entirely to toys and games and other means of play. It's both a children's museum and a museum of history, and it houses the **NATIONAL TOY HALL OF FAME** and the International Center for the History of Electronic Games.

Source: http://www.bmigaming.com, http://www.escapistmagazine.com, http://www.hasbro.com, http://www.museumofplay.org

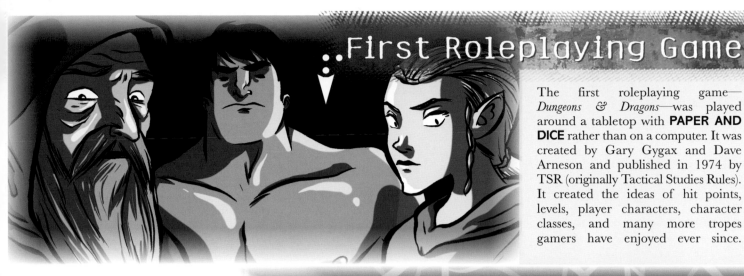

..First Roleplaying Game

The first roleplaying game—*Dungeons & Dragons*—was played around a tabletop with **PAPER AND DICE** rather than on a computer. It was created by Gary Gygax and Dave Arneson and published in 1974 by TSR (originally Tactical Studies Rules). It created the ideas of hit points, levels, player characters, character classes, and many more tropes gamers have enjoyed ever since.

Costliest Broadway Musical...

Producers of a musical based on Marvel Comics' hottest hero, called **SPIDER-MAN: TURN OFF THE DARK**, have already spent $65 million on putting the show together. While it features music from Bono and the Edge and some of the most spectacular stunts ever produced for a running show, it's struggled through several delays, including injured actors and stuntmen.

First TV Show

The first official, nonexperimental TV broadcasts in the U.S. that were sanctioned by the FCC aired on July 1, 1941. Two stations started simultaneously in New York City: WNBT (later WNBC) and WCBW (later WCBS). The first program covered a baseball game between the Brooklyn Dodgers and the Philadelphia Phillies. The first studio show was a game show called **TRUTH OR CONSEQUENCES**.

WHO'S GOT NEXT?

First Collectible Card Game

The first successful collectible card game was *Magic: The Gathering*, designed by Richard Garfield and published by Wizards of the Coast. It debuted in 1993 and became so successful that it spawned a professional tour that has awarded over **$30 MILLION IN PRIZES** and has had its finals broadcast on ESPN2.

First 3D Film

3D films are all the rage now, but the first feature film to be released in 3D was *The Power of Love*, **BACK IN 1922.** It used two cameras to create film shown with two projectors on the same screen at once. Viewers had to wear glasses with one lens tinted green and the other red. Sadly, the film has been lost.

First Color TV

The first color TV sold commercially was the CBS-Columbia Color Television Receiver, which went on sale in 1951. It used **A SPINNING COLOR DISK** mounted in front of a black-and-white TV tube. The first color broadcast—of *The Ed Sullivan Show*—was on June 25th of that year, but fewer than 50 TVs could actually see it in color. That system was abandoned less than four months later.

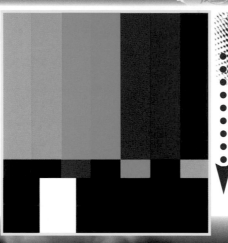

First Zombie Film

The first feature-length zombie movie ever made was *White Zombie*. It debuted in 1932, and it starred Bela Lugosi as Haitian voodoo master **MURDER LEGENDRE** and was directed by Victor Halperin. It features zombie slaves working in the fields rather than the brain-hungry kind, but it paved the way for all the zombie flicks to come.

Source: http://www.tvhistory.tv, http://www.3dgear.com, http://www.thehotspotonline.com

The Bestselling Album

The bestselling album of all time is Michael Jackson's **THRILLER**. Sales of his music spiked again after his death in 2009, and *Thriller* is now estimated to have sold around 110 million copies since its debut in 1982. That's twice as many as any of the closest runners-up.

First Vampire Film

The first vampire film wasn't *Dracula* but *Nosferatu*, an unauthorized rip-off of Bram Stoker's *Dracula* novel. This silent film came out in 1922, nine years before the official *Dracula* film, and it starred Max Shreck as the ugly and evil **Count Orlok**. Stoker's widow sued to have the film destroyed, but copies survived, and a definitive restoration was released in 1995.

....Most-Watched TV Show

The TV show that garnered the most viewers ever in the U.S. was the **AMERICAN TV DEBUT OF THE BEATLES.** That February 9, 1964, episode of *The Ed Sullivan Show* drew an audience of 73 million people. At the time, that was about 45% of the nation.

Longest-Running Children's Show

The kids' show that's been on TV for the longest is *Sesame Street* by a mile. It started out on November 10, 1969, and that original episode was "sponsored by the letters W, S, and E and the numbers 2 and 3." The same actor—**CARROLL SPINNEY,** who has been with the show since the beginning—still plays both Big Bird and Oscar the Grouch.

Biggest Movie Ever

The film that's made the most money worldwide is James Cameron's **AVATAR**, which will have raked in over $3 billion before it's done with theaters. However, if you adjust for 60 years of inflation, the biggest movie ever in the U.S. is Victor Fleming's *Gone With the Wind*, which nearly doubled *Avatar's* numbers.

Largest Group Playing DS

The world record for the largest group of Nintendo DS players getting their game on all at once is officially 580, as set in at the MCM Expo in London in May 2010. However, the previous September at the Penny Arcade Expo in Seattle, a reported 910 people gathered to do the same, but the record could not be verified.

Beautiful Pixels

In 2010, Lara Croft—heroine of the hit series of *Tomb Raider* games—broke the record for the highest-resolution video game character ever. In *Tomb Raider: Underworld*, artists used **32,816 POLYGONS** to render her model, the most ever used in any commercial game. We've come a long way since Ms. Pac-Man.

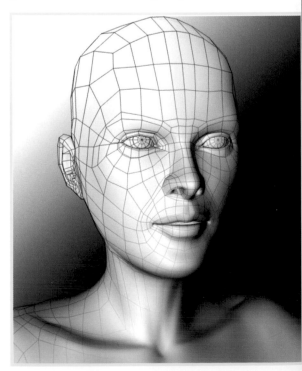

Source: http://www.boxofficemojo.com, http://nymag.com, http://www.worldamazingrecords.com, http://www.crofttimes.com

...Old News

The oldest continuously published newspaper in the U.S. is the *Hartford Courant*, which began in 1764 as the *Connecticut Courant*. It started out as a weekly paper, though, and has only been a daily since 1837. Because of that, the *New York Post*, which launched in 1801 under **ALEXANDER HAMILTON**, is the nation's oldest daily paper.

..Bestselling Book

The bestselling book of all time is far and away the Bible. An estimated 2.5 billion have been sold. The bestselling novel of all time seems to be *A Tale of Two Cities* by Charles Dickens, with over 200 million sold. The bestselling novel of the last hundred years is **J. R. R. TOLKIEN'S** *THE LORD OF THE RINGS*, which has sold over 150 million.

Hottest Video Games Ever..

The bestselling video game of all time is **WII SPORTS,** which sold more than 66 million copies. Of course, much of that comes from the fact that every Wii sold everywhere but Japan came packed with a copy of *Wii Sports.* For games that didn't come with a console, *Wii Play* is the winner with over 27 million copies but that came with a Wii remote.

Most Expensive Game

Grand Theft Auto IV holds the title for the biggest development budget ever for a video game at $100 million, but it sold at retail for only $60. The game that costs the most to buy is the **JEWEL ROYALE CHESS SET**, which features pieces made in gold and platinum and set with diamonds and other precious stones. It's worth roughly $7.75 million.

Biggest Bet

When Ashley Revell bet $135,300 on one spin of a roulette wheel, it wasn't the largest bet ever made, but it was everything to him. **HE'D SOLD EVERYTHING HE OWNED,** including his clothes, to raise the cash. He bet it all on red, and that's what came up, doubling his money. He then did the smart thing: pocketed the money and left the casino behind.

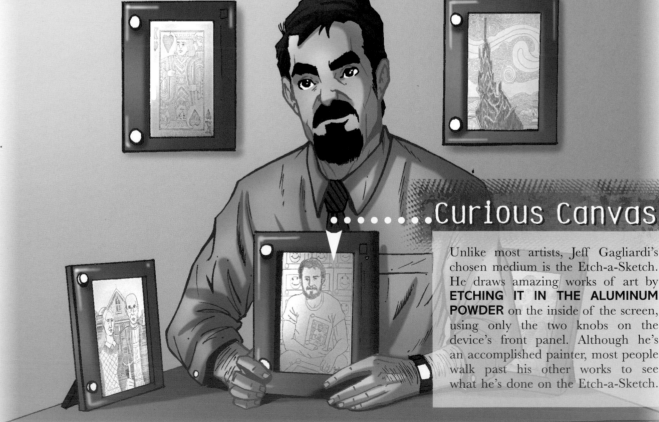

Curious Canvas

Unlike most artists, Jeff Gagliardi's chosen medium is the Etch-a-Sketch. He draws amazing works of art by **ETCHING IT IN THE ALUMINUM POWDER** on the inside of the screen, using only the two knobs on the device's front panel. Although he's an accomplished painter, most people walk past his other works to see what he's done on the Etch-a-Sketch.

Source: http://articles.ccn.com, http://www.digitalbattle.com, http://www.chessville.com, http://www.etch-a-sketchartist.com

...Loudest Band in the World

The heavy metal band Manowar holds the record for the loudest sounds ever played by a band. During a sound check before the Magic Circle Festival in Bad Arolsen, Germany, in 2008, they cranked it up to **MORE THAN 139 DECIBELS,** well over the standard pain-inducing level of 120.

Most Popular Video Game Console

Today's electronic gamer has lots of devices to choose from: Xbox 360, PlayStation 3, Wii, Nintendo DS, PSP, and a slew of smartphones like the iPhone or the Android, not to mention using a Mac or a PC. The bestselling gaming console of all time, though, is still the **PLAYSTATION 2,** which has sold over 140 million units worldwide.

NEWS YOU CAN USE

Keeping Detroit in Business

At the time of its release in 1980, *The Blues Brothers* held the record for the most cars destroyed in the making of a single film, including 11 of the 12 different versions of the Bluesmobile. The only film to ever break that record was *The Blues Brothers 2000,* which **CRASHED 60 CARS** into each other in a single pile-up.

Bestselling Trading Card Game

The bestselling trading card game in the world is not *Magic: The Gathering* or *Pokémon* but *Yu-Gi-Oh!* Since its release in Japan in 1999, it has sold over **22 BILLION CARDS** around the world. That's enough for everyone on the planet to have at least 3 cards of their very own.

Biggest Concert Ever

When Rod Stewart helped ring in New Year's Eve in Rio de Janeiro, Brazil, at the end of 1994, he set up the show on the Copacabana Beach rather than in a stadium. He also made the show free for anyone who cared to attend. Roughly **3.5 MILLION PEOPLE** showed up to count down to 1995 with him.

...Highest-Grossing Concert Tour

Re-establishing themselves as the greatest rock and roll band of all time, the Rolling Stones shattered all previous records for the highest-grossing concert tour ever with their 2005 to 2007 tour, "A Bigger Bang." The take from 144 shows came to a grand total of over **$558 MILLION.**

Biggest Game Show Jackpot

The biggest winner for any game show ever is Brad Rutter, who's won over $3.2 million over several appearances on *Jeopardy*. He stole the crown from Ken Jennings, who'd won $2.5 million on the same show in 2004, plus another half million in 2005. Jennings then regained the crown for total game show winnings by taking on other game shows, making his total **$3.6 MILLION.**

NEWS YOU CAN USE

Most Popular MMO

The most popular massively multiplayer online game is *World Of Warcraft*, which peaked in 2009 with 12 million subscribers. *RuneScape* is the most popular free MMO in the world with over **150 MILLION ACCOUNTS CREATED** since its launch in 2001. For Facebook games, *Farmville* is the big winner with over 80 million monthly active players at its height.

Source: http://www.askmen.com, http://www.billboard.com, http://www.celebritynetworth.com, http://mmodata.blogspot.com

First Home Video Game Console

The first video game console sold for use in homes was the **MAGNAVOX ODYSSEY,** which debuted in 1972, three years before Atari launched Pong. It came with two controllers, six game cartridges, and colored plastic overlays to tape onto your TV set. It even shipped with play money and dice!

No. 1   JUNE, 1938

ACTION COMICS

10¢

"Action Comics" #1 courtesy of DC Comics.

The Fight Over the First Superhero

The first superhero—as we know them, with superpowers, costumes, and secret identities—was **SUPERMAN,** who debuted in Action Comics #1 back in June 1938. Jerry Siegel and Joe Shuster created him and sold him to DC Comics, but in recent years their heirs have sued to win back the rights to the character.

Most Valuable Comic

The most valuable comic in the world is *Action Comics #1,* which features the premiere of Superman. In March 2010, a copy of it sold for **$1.5 million.** In 2009, the record for the highest price ever paid for a comic (another copy of *Action Comics #1*) was a mere $317,000. Originally, these comics sold for 10¢, but only about 100 copies of that issue remain.

UNBREAKABLE

Bestselling Comic

The bestselling comic book of all time is *X-Men #1,* a relaunch of the ever-popular *X-Men.* Written by Chris Claremont and drawn by **JIM LEE,** the comic sold a stunning 7 million copies at the height of the '90s comic boom. Lee went on to found a part of Image Comics called WildStorm, which he later sold to DC Comics. Recently, Lee became DC's co-publisher.

Speculative Writing

Screenwriters often write a script on spec (speculating that they will sell it at some point) and then shop it around Hollywood. It's like writing your own lottery ticket. The biggest payoff for any such script was $5 million for **DÉJÀ VU,** written by Terry Rossio and Bill Marsilii.

Highest-Paid Gamer

South Korea actually has full leagues of professional gaming teams who play in televised events, and their greatest competitions are over *Starcraft* and *Warcraft III*. In 2007, **LEE YOON "NADA" YEOL** signed a contract with WeMade FOX worth over $625,000, making him the highest-paid gamer in history.

Highest-Paid TV Star

A lot of people make a lot of money in television, but none of them even come close to the queen of daytime TV, **OPRAH WINFREY,** who makes roughly $385 million dollars a year. Having accumulated a net worth of over $2.5 billion, she's built an unstoppable entertainment empire.

Source: http://highest-paid.net, http://www.gosugamers.net

Biggest Book

The world's biggest book is a massive installation of **730 DOUBLE-SIDED MARBLE LEAVES (1,460 PAGES)**, each of which stands five feet tall, three and a half feet wide, and five inches thick and sits under its own protective stone pagoda. The text carved on the pages contains the Pali canon, the scriptures of Theravada Buddhism. King Mindon of Burma had it built in the 1860s.

The Most Expensive Die

A 20-sided die made out of blue-green glass was found in Egypt in the 1920s. It featured Roman etchings on its faces, and it was dated to sometime in the **2ND CENTURY AD.** It was put up for auction at Christie's in 2003, and it sold for $17,925. No one knows what the die was used for, but today's 20-sided dice are used mostly in role-playing games like *Dungeons & Dragons!*

$17,925

The Oldest Game

Many games claim to be the oldest in the world, but the one with the best evidence to back that up is the board game **SENET**, which was played in Egypt at least as far back as 3100 BC. Backgammon makes a good case for being the oldest too, as the oldest Backgammon board found dates to around 3000 BC!

Source: http://www.kuriositas.com, http://www.tradgames.org.uk, http://www.christies.com

GET IN THE ACTION!

Why just read the **BOOK OF EXTREME FACTS** when you can be featured in it yourself? Perhaps this chapter has inspired you to set or share some records of your own, such as:

• Marathon RPG gaming sessions!
• Video game records that prove you are master of the console!
• Outstanding achievements in art, music, or theater!

Remember, you are not limited to the above suggestions, or to trying to beat other records in this chapter. Entirely new records are not only allowed… they are encouraged! The only limit is your own creativity. So have some fun (but always remember to keep it SAFE), and if you are younger than 18 remember to ask your parents for permission before attempting any record.

To submit a record:

-Go to *www.bookofextremefacts.com*

-Click on the "Submit New Record" tab

-Provide a brief description of your record and your contact info

-If we decide that your record makes the grade, we will contact you for further details and photos or video of your record

It's just that simple! Good luck…
and **KEEP IT EXTREME!**

Involvement in dangerous sports and related activities carries a significant risk of damage to property, personal injury or death. Please do not endanger yourself or others or take any unnecessary risks. If you choose to participate in dangerous sports or activities in attempting to achieve a distinction that would be recognized in the next edition of Extreme Facts, which IDW does not recommend, you do so at your own risk. IDW suggests the use of professional instruction before entering into any sports or physical activity. You should become knowledgeable about the risks involved. By submitting information to IDW related to inclusion in a future edition of Extreme Facts you assume personal responsibility for your actions and agree to indemnify and hold harmless IDW for the consequences of your actions.

IMAGE CREDITS

Page 158 - FIRST COLOR TV Photo by Denelson83
Page 160 - BIGGEST MOVIE EVER Photo by William Hook
Page 160 - BEAUTIFUL PIXELS Photo by Geierunited
Page 164 - BIGGEST CONCERT EVER Photo by Mike Vondran
Page 166 - HIGHEST-PAID GAMER Photo by Seung Hyun Park
Page 166 - HIGHEST-PAID TV STAR Photo by Alan Light